GREAT
CHICKEN
DISHES

GREAT CHICKEN DISHES

PERFECT POULTRY AND GOURMET GAME DISHES

Consultant Editor: Linda Fraser

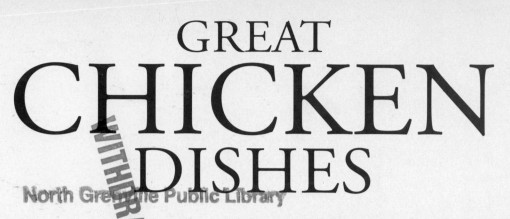

HERMES HOUSE

This edition produced in 2001 by Hermes House

©Anness Publishing Ltd 2001
Anness Publishing Limited
Hermes House
88–89 Blackfriars Road
London SE1 8HA

© 2001 Anness Publishing Limited

A CIP catalogue record for this book is available from the British Library

Publisher: Joanna Lorenz
Senior Cookery Editor: Linda Fraser
Designers: Tony Paine and Roy Prescott
Photographers: Steve baxter, Karl Adamson and Amanda Heywood
Food for photography: Wendy Lee, Jane Stevenson and Elizabeth Wolf Cohen
Props Stylists: Blake Minton, assisted by Kirsty Rawlings
Additional recipes: Carla Capalbo and Laura Washburn

Front cover: Nicki Dowey, Photographer and Stylist;
Emma Patmore, Home Economist

Previously published as part of the *Creative Cooking Library*

Printed and bound in Hong Kong/China

1 3 5 7 9 10 8 6 4 2

MEASUREMENTS
For all recipes, quantities are given in both metric and imperial measures and,
where appropriate, measures are also given in standard cups and spoons. Follow
one set, but not a mixture because they are not interchangeable.

Medium eggs should be used unless otherwise stated.

 The apple symbol indicates a low fat, low cholesterol recipe.

CONTENTS

Introduction *6*

Light Lunches *12*

Dinner Party Dishes *44*

Roasts, Pies and Hot-pots *70*

Index *96*

POULTRY PREPARATION – TIPS AND TECHNIQUES

Chicken and other birds are a mainstay of weekday meals, holiday gatherings and festive occasions. Knowing how to handle poultry helps you to make the most of it. Here we give you all the information you need from trussing and roasting through to preparing perfect stocks and sauces.

TRUSSING POULTRY

Trussing holds a bird together during cooking so that it keeps a neat, attractive shape. If the bird is stuffed, trussing prevents the stuffing falling out. You can truss with strong string or with poultry skewers.

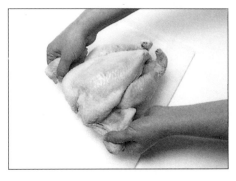

1 **For an unstuffed bird**: set it breast down and pull the flap of neck skin over the neck opening. Turn the bird breast up and fold each wing tip back, over the neck skin, to secure firmly behind the shoulder.

2 Press the legs firmly down and into the breast. If there is a band of skin across the parson's nose, fold back the ends of the drumsticks and tuck them under the skin.

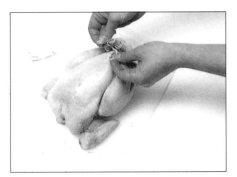

3 Otherwise, cross the knuckle ends of the drumsticks or bring them tightly together. Loop a length of string several times around the drumstick ends, then tie a knot and trim off the excess string.

4 **For a stuffed bird**: fold the wing tips back as above. After stuffing the neck end, fold the flap of skin over the opening and secure it with a skewer, then fold over the wing tips.

5 Put any stuffing or flavourings (herbs, lemon halves, apple quarters and so on) in the body cavity, then secure the ends of the drumsticks as above, tying in the parson's nose, too.

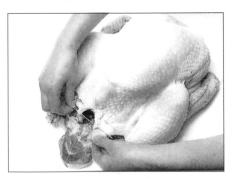

6 Alternatively, the cavity opening can be closed with skewers: insert two or more skewers across the opening, threading them through the skin several times.

7 Lace the skewers together with string. Tie the drumsticks together over the skewers.

STUFFING TIPS

When stuffing poultry, the stuffing should be cool, not hot or chilled. Pack it loosely into the bird because it will expand during cooking. Cook any left-over stuffing separately in a baking dish. Do not stuff poultry until just before putting it into the oven or pot. It is not a good idea to stuff the body cavity of a large bird because the stuffing could inhibit heat penetration, and thus not kill all harmful bacteria.

ROASTING POULTRY

Where would family gatherings be without the time-honoured roast bird? But beyond the favourite chicken, all types of poultry can be roasted – from small poussins to large turkeys. However, older tougher birds are better pot-roasted.

SIMPLE ROAST CHICKEN

Squeeze the juice from a halved lemon over a 1.35-1.5kg/3-3½lb chicken, then push the lemon halves into the body cavity. Smear 15g/½oz softened butter over the breast. Roast in a 190°C/375°F/Gas 5 oven for about 1¼ hours. Skim all fat from the roasting juices, then add 120ml/4fl oz water and bring to the boil, stirring well to mix in the browned bits. Season with salt and pepper, and serve this sauce with the chicken. *Serves 4.*

PROTECT AND FLAVOUR

Before roasting, loosen the skin on the breast by gently easing it away from the flesh with your fingers. Press in softened butter mixed with herbs or garlic for extra flavour – and carefully smooth back the skin.

1 Wipe the bird inside and out with damp paper towels. Stuff the bird if the recipe directs and truss it. Spread the breast of chicken with softened or melted butter or oil; bard the breast of a lean game bird; prick the skin of duck and goose.

2 Set the bird breast up on a rack in a small roasting tin or shallow baking dish. If you are roasting a lean game bird, set the bird in the tin breast down.

3 Roast the bird, basting it every 10 minutes after the first ½ hour with the accumulated juices and fat in the tin. Turn if directed. If browning too quickly, cover loosely with foil.

4 Transfer the bird to a carving board and leave to rest for at least 15 minutes before serving. During that time, make a simple sauce or gravy with the juices in the tin.

ROASTING TIMES FOR POULTRY

Note: Cooking times given here are for unstuffed birds. For stuffed birds, add 20 minutes to the total roasting time.

Poussin	450–700g/1-1½lb	1-1¼ hours at 180°C/350°F/Gas 4
Chicken	1.12-1.35kg/2½-3lb	1-1¼ hours at 190°C/375°F/Gas 5
	1.5-1.8kg/3½-4lb	1¼-1¾ hours at 190°C/375°F/Gas 5
	2-2.25kg/4½-5lb	1½-2 hours at 190°C/375°F/Gas 5
	2.25-2.7kg/5-6lb	1¾-2½ hours at 190°C/375°F/Gas 5
Duck	1.35-2.25kg/3-5lb	1¾-2¼ hours at 200°C/400°F/Gas 6
Goose	3.6-4.5kg/8-10lb	2½-3 hours at 180°C/350°F/Gas 4
	4.5-5.4kg/10-12lb	3-3½ hours at 180°C/350°F/Gas 4
Turkey	2.7-3.6kg/6-8lb	3-3½ hours at 170°C/325°F/Gas 3
(whole bird)	3.6-5.4kg/8-12lb	3-4 hours at 170°C/325°F/Gas 3
	5.4-7.2kg/12-16lb	4-5 hours at 170°C/325°F/Gas 3
Turkey	1.8-2.7kg/4-6lb	1½-2¼ hours at 170°C/325°F/Gas 3
(whole breast)	2.7-3.6kg/6-8lb	2¼-3¼ hours at 170°C/325°F/Gas 3

PREPARING DUCK AND GOOSE FOR ROASTING

Duck and goose are bony birds, with most of their rich meat in the breast. There is a thick layer of fat under the skin which should be removed before cooking or melted out during cooking.

LEAN BY NATURE

Wild duck and geese should be prepared as you would a game bird so the meat doesn't dry out: bard the breast with rashers of bacon.

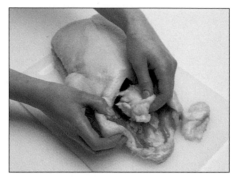

1 Pull out any fat from the body and neck cavities. Prick the skin all over the breast of the bird.

2 Tie the ends of the drumsticks together with string as for a chicken.

CARVING POULTRY

Carving a bird neatly for serving makes the presentation attractive. You will need a sharp long-bladed knife, or an electric knife, plus a long two-pronged fork and a carving board with a well to catch the juices.

Cut away any trussing string. For a stuffed bird, spoon the stuffing from the cavity into a serving dish. For easier carving, remove the wishbone.

Insert the fork into one breast to hold the bird steady. Cut through the skin to the ball an socket joint on that side of the body, then slice through it to sever the leg from the body. Repeat on the other side.

1 Slice through the ball and socket joint in each leg to sever the thigh and drumstick. If carving turkey, slice the meat off the thigh and drumstick, parallel to the bone, turning to get even slices; leave chicken thighs and drumsticks whole.

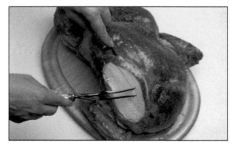

2 To carve the breast of a turkey or chicken, cut 3–5mm/⅛–¼in thick slices at an angle, slicing down on both sides of the breastbone. For smaller birds, remove the meat on each side of the breastbone in a single piece, then slice thinly across the grain.

PREPARING TURKEY ESCALOPES

Escalopes are slices cut crossways from the turkey breast. Economical and extremely versatile, they are a lean meat that cooks quickly and can be used as a substitute in most recipes that call for veal escalopes. Turkey escalopes can also be treated in much the same way as thin beef or pork steaks, or used in place of chicken breast fillets.

Slicing across the grain ensures that the escalope won't shrink or curl when it is cooked, and cutting on the diagonal gives good-sized slices.

1 With a large sharp knife, cut the boned breast across the grain, at a slight angle, into 1cm/⅜in slices.

2 Put each slice between two sheets of greaseproof paper and pound lightly with the base of a pan to flatten.

BONING CHICKEN AND TURKEY BREASTS

Boneless poultry breasts, both whole and halves, are widely available, but they tend to be more expensive than breasts with bone. So it is more economical to bone the breasts yourself, and it is really very easy to do. A thin-bladed boning knife is the ideal tool to use.

TERMS FOR CHICKEN BREASTS

Boneless chicken breasts are often called fillets. If the wing is attached, they are usually known as suprêmes.

1 **To take two boneless breasts from a whole breast**: first pull off the skin and any loose fat. Then with the knife, cut through the breast meat along both sides of the ridged top of the breastbone.

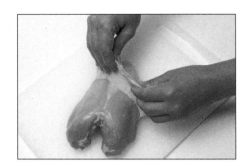

2 With the knife at an angle, scrape the meat away from the bone down one side of the rib cage. Do this carefully so the breast meat comes away in one neat piece. Repeat on the other side. You now have two skinless boneless breasts.

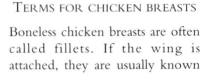

3 **To remove the meat from a breast**: if the wing is attached, cut through the ball and socket joint to separate the wing and breast. (Keep the wing for stock or another use.) Pull off the skin, if desired.

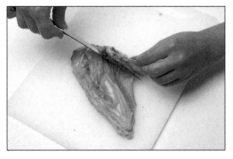

4 Turn the breast over and scrape the meat from the bone, using short strokes and lifting away the bone as it is freed.

5 Before cooking, remove the tendon next to the long flap or fillet on the underside of the breast. Cut it free of the meat at one end and pull it away, scraping it gently with the knife to remove it neatly.

6 Trim any fat from the breast. Put it between two sheets of clear film or greaseproof paper and pound lightly with a meat mallet, the base of a saucepan or a rolling pin to flatten the breast slightly.

7 **To bone a whole breast for stuffing**: you must keep the skin intact. Set the breast skin side down and scrape the meat away from the rib cage, starting at one side and working up to the ridged top of the breastbone. Repeat on the other side.

8 When the meat has been freed on both sides, lift up the rib cage and scrape the skin gently away from both sides of the top of the breastbone, taking care not to cut through the skin. The breast is now boned in one piece.

JOINTING POULTRY

Although chickens and other poultry are sold already jointed into halves, quarters, breasts, thighs and drumsticks, sometimes it makes sense to buy a whole bird and to do the job yourself. That way you can prepare four larger pieces or eight smaller ones, depending on the recipe, and you can cut the pieces so the backbone and other bony bits (which can be saved for stock) are not included. In addition, a whole bird is cheaper to buy than pieces.

A sharp knife and sturdy kitchen scissors or poultry shears make the job of jointing poultry very easy.

SAFE HANDLING OF RAW POULTRY

Raw poultry may harbour potentially harmful organisms, such as salmonella bacteria, so it is vital to take care in its preparation. Always wash your hands, the chopping board, knife and poultry shears in hot soapy water before and after handling the poultry. It is a good idea to use a chopping board that can be washed in a dishwasher and, if possible, to keep the chopping board just for the preparation of raw poultry. Thaw frozen poultry completely before cooking.

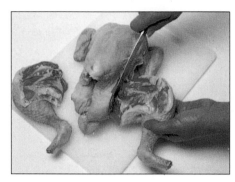

1 With the sharp knife, cut through the skin on one side of the body down to where the thigh joins the body. Bend the leg out away from the body and twist it to break the ball and socket joint.

2 Hold the leg out away from the body and cut through the ball and socket joint, taking the 'oyster meat' from the backbone with the leg. Repeat on the other side.

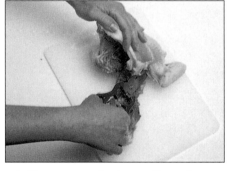

3 To separate the breast from the back, cut through the flap of skin just below the rib cage, cutting towards the neck. Pull the breast and back apart and cut through the joints that connect them on each side. Reserve the back for stock.

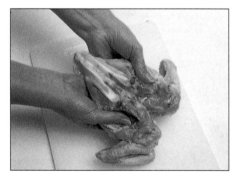

4 Turn the whole breast over, skin side down. Take one side of the breast in each hand and bend back firmly so the breastbone pops free. Loosen the bone on both sides with your fingers and, with the help of the knife, remove it.

5 Cut the breast lengthways in half, cutting through the wishbone. You now have two breasts with wings attached and two leg portions.

6 For eight pieces, cut each breast in half at an angle so that some breast meat is included with a wing portion. Trim off any protruding bones.

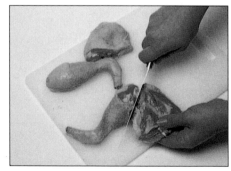

7 With the knife, cut each leg portion through the ball and socket joint to separate the thigh and drumstick.

MAKING POULTRY STOCK

A good home-made poultry stock is invaluable in the kitchen. It is simple and economical to make, and can be stored in the freezer for up to six months. If poultry giblets are available, add them to the stockpot (except the livers) with the wings.

Makes about 2.5 litres/4 pints
1.12–1.35kg/2½–3lb poultry wings, backs and necks (chicken, turkey, etc)
2 onions, unpeeled and quartered
4 litres/6½ pints cold water
2 carrots, roughly chopped
2 celery stalks, with leaves if possible, roughly chopped
a small handful of fresh parsley
a few fresh thyme sprigs or 5ml/1tsp dried thyme
1 or 2 bay leaves
10 black peppercorns, lightly crushed

A FRUGAL STOCK

Stock can be made from the bones and carcasses of roasted poultry, cooked with vegetables and flavourings. Save the carcasses in a polythene bag in the freezer until you have three or four, then make stock. It may not have quite as rich a flavour as stock made from a whole bird or fresh wings, backs and necks, but it will still taste fresher and less salty than stock made from a cube.

1 Combine the poultry wings, backs and necks and the onions in a stockpot. Cook over moderate heat, stirring occasionally so they colour evenly, until lightly browned.

3 Add the remaining ingredients. Partly cover the stockpot and gently simmer the stock for 3 hours.

5 When cold, remove the layer of fat that will have set on the surface.

2 Add the water and stir well to mix in the sediment on the bottom of the pot. Bring to the boil and skim off the impurities as they rise to the surface of the stock.

4 Strain the stock into a bowl and leave to cool, then refrigerate.

STOCK TIPS

If wished, use a whole bird for making stock instead of wings, backs and necks. A boiling fowl will give wonderful flavour and provide plenty of chicken meat to use in soups and casseroles.

No salt is added to stock because as the stock reduces the flavour becomes concentrated and saltiness increases. Add salt to the dish in which the stock is used.

LIGHT LUNCHES

Meals in the middle of the day are often rushed affairs mid-week, so there are plenty of quick-to-prepare recipes here, such as Turkey Strips with Soured Cream Dip, or Thai Chicken and Vegetable Stir-fry. At the weekend, when there's more time to spare, try one of the marinated chicken dishes: Spatchcocked Devilled Poussin is perfect if you are entertaining, while Minted Yogurt Chicken makes a delicious low fat family lunch.

Spatchcocked Devilled Poussin

'Spatchcock', perhaps a corruption of the old Irish phrase 'despatch a cock', refers to birds that are split and skewered flat for cooking.

INGREDIENTS

Serves 4

15ml/1 tbsp English mustard powder
15ml/1 tbsp paprika
15ml/1 tbsp ground cumin
20ml/4 tsp tomato ketchup
15ml/1 tbsp lemon juice
65g/2½oz/5 tbsp butter, melted
4 poussins, about 450g/1lb each
salt

1 Mix together the mustard, paprika, cumin, ketchup, lemon juice and salt until smooth, then gradually stir in the butter.

2 Using game shears or strong kitchen scissors, split each poussin along one side of the backbone, then cut down the other side of the back-bone to remove it.

3 Open out a poussin, skin side uppermost, then press down firmly with the heel of your hand. Pass a long skewer through one leg and out through the other to secure the bird open and flat. Repeat with the remaining birds.

4 Spread the mustard mixture evenly over the skin of the birds. Cover loosely and leave in a cool place for at least 2 hours. Preheat the grill.

5 Place the birds, skin side upper-most, under the grill and cook for about 12 minutes. Turn the birds over, baste with any juices in the pan, and cook for a further 7 minutes, until the juices run clear.

COOK'S TIP

Spatchcocked poussin cook very well on the barbecue, make sure the coals are very hot, then cook for 15–20 minutes, turning and basting frequently.

Cajun Chicken Jambalaya

INGREDIENTS

Serves 4

1.25kg/2½lb fresh chicken
1½ onions
1 bay leaf
4 black peppercorns
1 parsley sprig
30ml/2 tbsp vegetable oil
2 garlic cloves, chopped
1 green pepper, seeded and chopped
1 celery stick, chopped
225g/8oz/1¼ cups long grain rice
115g/4oz/1 cup Chorizo sausage, sliced
115g/4oz/1 cup chopped, cooked ham
400g/14oz can chopped tomatoes with
  herbs
2.5ml/½ tsp hot chilli powder
2.5ml/½ tsp cumin seeds
2.5ml/½ tsp ground cumin
5ml/1 tsp dried thyme
115g/4oz/1 cup cooked, peeled prawns
dash of Tabasco sauce
chopped parsley, to garnish

1 Place the chicken in a large flame-proof casserole and pour over 600ml/1 pint/2½ cups water. Add the half onion, the bay leaf, peppercorns and parsley and bring to the boil. Cover and simmer gently for about 1½ hours.

2 When the chicken is cooked lift it out of the stock, remove the skin and carcass and chop the meat. Strain the stock, leave to cool and reserve.

3 Chop the remaining onion and heat the oil in a large frying pan. Add the onion, garlic, green pepper and celery. Fry for about 5 minutes, then stir in the rice coating the grains with the oil. Add the sausage, ham and reserved chopped chicken and fry for a further 2–3 minutes, stirring frequently.

4 Pour in the tomatoes and 300ml/ ½ pint/1¼ cups of the reserved stock and add the chilli, cumin, and thyme. Bring to the boil, then cover and simmer gently for 20 minutes, or until the rice is tender and the liquid absorbed.

5 Stir in the prawns and Tabasco. Cook for a further 5 minutes, then season well and serve hot garnished with chopped parsley.

Turkey Sticks with Soured Cream Dip

INGREDIENTS

Serves 4
350g/12oz turkey fillets, or 2 boneless
   breast portions
50g/2oz/1 cup fine fresh breadcrumbs
1.25ml/¼ tsp paprika
1 size 4 egg, lightly beaten
45ml/3 tbsp soured cream
15ml/1 tbsp ready-made tomato
   sauce
15ml/1 tbsp mayonnaise
salt and black pepper

1 Preheat the oven to 190°C/375°F/
Gas 5. Cut the turkey into strips.
Mix the breadcrumbs with paprika and
season with salt and pepper.

2 Dip the turkey into the egg, then
into the breadcrumbs, until thoroughly and evenly coated. Place on a
baking sheet when they are prepared.

3 Cook the turkey at the top of the
oven for 20 minutes, until crisp and
golden. Turn once during cooking.

4 To make the dip, mix the soured
cream, tomato sauce and mayonnaise together in a small bowl and
season to taste. Serve the turkey sticks
with baked potatoes and a green salad
or crisp green vegetables, accompanied
by the dip.

Chicken, Bacon and Corn Kebabs

Don't wait for barbecue weather to
have kebabs. If you are serving
them to children, remember to
remove the kebab sticks first.

INGREDIENTS

Serves 4
2 corn-on-the-cob, cooked
8 thick rashers back bacon
8 brown cap mushrooms, halved
2 small chicken fillets
30ml/2 tbsp sunflower oil
15ml/1 tbsp lemon juice
15ml/1 tbsp maple syrup
salt and black pepper

1 Cook the corn in boiling water
until tender, then drain and cool.
Stretch the bacon rashers with the back
of a knife; cut each in half. Wrap a
piece around each half mushroom.

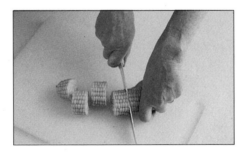

2 Cut both the corn and chicken into
eight equal pieces. Mix together the
oil, lemon juice, syrup and seasoning
and brush liberally over the chicken.

3 Thread the corn, bacon-wrapped
mushrooms and chicken pieces
alternately on skewers and brush all
over with the lemon dressing.

4 Grill for 8–10 minutes,
turning them once and basting
occasionally with any extra dressing.
Serve hot with either a crisp green or
mixed leaf salad.

Turkey Pastitsio

A traditional Greek pastitsio is a rich, high-fat dish made with minced beef, but this lighter version is just as tasty.

INGREDIENTS 🍎

Serves 4–6

450g/1lb lean minced turkey
1 large onion, finely chopped
60ml/4 tbsp tomato purée
250ml/8fl oz/1 cup red wine or stock
5ml/1 tsp ground cinnamon
300g/11oz/2½ cups macaroni
300ml/½ pint/1¼ cups skimmed milk
25g/1oz/2 tbsp sunflower margarine
25g/1oz/3 tbsp plain flour
5ml/1 tsp ground nutmeg
2 tomatoes, sliced
60ml/4 tbsp wholemeal breadcrumbs
salt and black pepper
green salad, to serve

1 Preheat the oven to 220°C/425°F/ Gas 7. Cook the turkey and chopped onion in a nonstick pan without fat, stirring until lightly browned.

2 Stir in the tomato purée, red wine or stock, and cinnamon. Season, then cover and simmer for 5 minutes.

3 Cook the macaroni in boiling, salted water until just tender, then drain. Layer with the meat mixture in a wide ovenproof dish.

4 Place the milk, margarine, and flour in a saucepan and whisk over a moderate heat until thickened and smooth. Add the nutmeg, and salt and pepper to taste.

5 Pour the sauce evenly over the pasta and meat. Arrange the tomato slices on top and sprinkle lines of breadcrumbs over the surface.

6 Bake for 30–35 minutes, or until golden brown and bubbling. Serve hot, with a green salad.

COOK'S TIP

If you can't find minced turkey, use minced chicken instead. If you are not too worried about the fat content then try this dish with minced lamb or beef.

Chicken with Herbs and Lentils

If your family don't like lentils (and some children don't) use rice instead.

INGREDIENTS

Serves 4

115g/4oz piece of thick bacon or belly pork, rind removed, chopped
1 large onion, sliced
450ml/¾ pint/1¼ cups well-flavoured chicken stock
bay leaf
2 sprigs each parsley, marjoram and thyme
225g/8oz/2 cups green or brown lentils
4 chicken portions
salt and black pepper
25–50g/1–2oz/2–4 tbsp garlic butter

1 Fry the bacon gently in a large, heavy-based flameproof casserole until all the fat runs out and the bacon begins to brown. Add the onions and fry for another 2 minutes.

2 Stir in the stock, bay leaf, herb stalks and some of the leafy parts (keep some herb sprigs for garnish), lentils and seasoning. Preheat the oven to 190°C/375°F/Gas 5.

3 Fry the chicken portions in a frying pan to brown the skin before placing on top of the lentils. Sprinkle with seasoning and some of the herbs.

4 Cover the casserole and cook in the oven for about 40 minutes. Serve with a knob of garlic butter on each portion of chicken and a few of the remaining herb sprigs scattered over.

COOK'S TIP

For economy buy a smallish roasting chicken and cut it in quarters, to give you four good-sized portions.

Chilli-Chicken Couscous

Couscous is a very easy alternative to rice and makes a good base for all kinds of ingredients.

INGREDIENTS 🍎

Serves 4

225g/8oz/2 cups couscous
1 litre/1¾ pints/4 cups boiling water
5ml/1 tsp olive oil
400g/14oz chicken without skin and
  bone, diced
1 yellow pepper, seeded and sliced
2 large courgettes, sliced thickly
1 small green chilli, thinly sliced, or
  1 tsp chilli sauce
1 large tomato, diced
425g/15oz can chick-peas, drained
salt and black pepper
coriander or parsley sprigs, to garnish

1 Place the couscous in a large bowl and pour over the boiling water. Cover and leave to stand for about 30 minutes.

2 Heat the oil in a large, non-stick pan and stir-fry the chicken quickly to seal, then reduce the heat.

3 Stir in the pepper, courgettes, and chilli or sauce and cook for 10 minutes, until the vegetables are softened.

4 Stir in the tomato and chick-peas, then add the couscous. Adjust the seasoning and stir over moderate heat until hot. Serve garnished with sprigs of fresh coriander or parsley.

VARIATION

There's no need to stick exactly to the recipe, you could use whatever vegetables you have to hand – try fine green beans, peas or broad beans in place of the courgettes.

Turkey and Bean Bake

INGREDIENTS 🍎

Serves 4

1 medium aubergine, thinly sliced
15ml/1 tbsp olive oil, for brushing
450g/1lb turkey breast, diced
1 medium onion, chopped
425g/14oz can chopped tomatoes
425g/15oz can red kidney beans, drained
15ml/1 tbsp paprika
15ml/1 tbsp fresh chopped thyme, or
  5ml/1 tsp dried
5ml/1 tsp chilli sauce
350g/12oz/1½ cups natural yogurt
2.5ml/½ tsp ground nutmeg
salt and black pepper

1 Preheat the oven to 190°C/375°F/ Gas 5. Arrange the aubergine in a colander and sprinkle with salt.

2 Leave the aubergine for 30 minutes, then rinse and pat dry. Brush a non-stick pan with oil and cook the aubergine in batches, turning once, until golden.

3 Remove the aubergine, add the turkey and onion to the pan, then cook until lightly browned. Stir in the tomatoes, beans, paprika, thyme, chilli sauce, and salt and pepper. In a separate bowl, mix together the yogurt and ground nutmeg.

4 Layer the meat and aubergine in an ovenproof dish, finishing with aubergine. Spread over the yogurt and bake for 50–60 minutes, until golden.

COOK'S TIP

Make sure that you dry the aubergine slices very thoroughly before frying. Squeeze them between sheets of kitchen paper – the drier the aubergine is, the less oil it will absorb.

Chinese-style Chicken Salad

INGREDIENTS

Serves 4

4 boneless chicken breasts (about 175g/6oz each)
60ml/4 tbsp dark soy sauce
pinch of Chinese five spice powder
a good squeeze of lemon juice
½ cucumber, peeled and cut into matchsticks
5ml/1 tsp salt
45ml/3 tbsp sunflower oil
30ml/2 tbsp sesame oil
15ml/1 tbsp sesame seeds
30ml/2 tbsp dry sherry
2 carrots, cut into matchsticks
8 spring onions, shredded
75g/3oz/1 cup beansprouts

For the sauce

60ml/4 tbsp crunchy peanut butter
10ml/2 tsp lemon juice
10ml/2 tsp sesame oil
1.25ml/¼ tsp hot chilli powder
1 spring onion, finely chopped

1 Put the chicken portions into a large pan and just cover with water. Add 15ml/1 tbsp of the soy sauce, the Chinese five spice powder and lemon juice, cover and bring to the boil, then simmer for about 20 minutes.

2 Meanwhile, place the cucumber matchsticks in a colander, sprinkle with the salt and cover with a plate with a weight on top. Leave to drain for 30 minutes — set the colander in a bowl or on a deep plate to catch the drips.

3 Lift out the poached chicken with a draining spoon and leave until cool enough to handle. Remove and discard the skins and bash the chicken lightly with a rolling pin to loosen the fibres. Slice into thin strips and reserve.

4 Heat the oils in a large frying pan or wok. Add the sesame seeds, fry for 30 seconds and then stir in the remaining 45ml/3 tbsp soy sauce and the sherry. Add the carrots and stir-fry for 2–3 minutes, until just tender. Remove from the heat and reserve.

5 Rinse the cucumber well, pat dry with kitchen paper and place in a bowl. Add the spring onions, beansprouts, cooked carrots, pan juices and shredded chicken, and mix together. Transfer to a shallow dish. Cover and chill for about 1 hour, turning the mixture in the juices once or twice.

6 To make the sauce, cream the peanut butter with the lemon juice, sesame oil and chilli powder, adding a little hot water to form a paste, then stir in the spring onion. Arrange the chicken mixture on a serving dish and serve with the peanut sauce.

Stir-fried Turkey with Mange-tout

INGREDIENTS

Serves 4

30ml/2 tbsp sesame oil
90ml/6 tbsp lemon juice
1 garlic clove, crushed
1cm/½in piece fresh root ginger,
  peeled and grated
5ml/1 tsp clear honey
450g/1lb turkey fillets, cut into strips
115g/4oz mange-tout, trimmed
30ml/2 tbsp groundnut oil
50g/2oz/⅓ cup cashew nuts
6 spring onions, cut into strips
225g/8oz can water chestnuts, drained
  and thinly sliced
salt
saffron rice, to serve

1 Mix together the sesame oil, lemon juice, garlic, ginger and honey in a shallow non-metallic dish. Add the turkey and mix well. Cover and leave to marinate for 3–4 hours.

2 Blanch the mange-tout in boiling salted water for 1 minute. Drain and refresh under cold running water.

3 Drain the marinade from the turkey strips and reserve the marinade. Heat the groundnut oil in a wok or large frying pan, add the cashew nuts and stir-fry for about 1–2 minutes until golden brown. Remove the cashew nuts from the wok or frying pan using a slotted spoon and set aside.

4 Add the turkey and stir-fry for 3–4 minutes, until golden brown. Add the spring onions, mange-tout, water chestnuts and the reserved marinade. Cook for a few minutes, until the turkey is tender and the sauce is bubbling and hot. Stir in the cashew nuts and serve with saffron rice.

Italian Chicken

INGREDIENTS

Serves 4

30ml/2 tbsp plain flour
4 chicken portions (legs, breasts or
    quarters)
30ml/2 tbsp olive oil
1 onion, chopped
2 garlic cloves, chopped
1 red pepper, seeded and chopped
400g/14oz can chopped tomatoes,
30ml/2 tbsp red pesto sauce
4 sun-dried tomatoes in oil, chopped
150ml/¼ pint/⅔ cup chicken stock
5ml/1 tsp dried oregano
8 black olives, stoned
salt and black pepper
chopped fresh basil and basil leaves,
    to garnish
tagliatelle, to serve

1 Place the flour and seasoning in a plastic bag. Add the chicken pieces and shake well until coated. Heat the oil in a flameproof casserole, add the chicken and brown quickly. Remove with a slotted spoon and set aside.

2 Lower the heat and add the onion, garlic and pepper and cook for 5 minutes. Stir in the remaining ingredients, except olives and bring to the boil.

3 Return the sautéed chicken portions to the casserole, season lightly, cover and simmer for 30–35 minutes, or until the chicken is cooked.

4 Add the olives and simmer for a further 5 minutes. Transfer to a warmed serving dish, sprinkle with the chopped basil and garnish with basil leaves. Serve with hot tagliatelle.

Honey and Orange Glazed Chicken

This way of cooking chicken breasts is popular in America, Australia and Great Britain. It is ideal for an easy evening meal served with baked potatoes.

INGREDIENTS

Serves 4

4 x 175g/6oz boneless chicken breasts
15ml/1 tbsp oil
4 spring onions, chopped
1 garlic clove, crushed
45ml/3 tbsp clear honey
60ml/4 tbsp fresh orange juice
1 orange, peeled and segmented
30ml/2 tbsp soy sauce
fresh lemon balm or flat leaf parsley,
    to garnish
baked potatoes and mixed salad, to
    serve

1 Preheat the oven to 190°C/375°F/ Gas 5. Place the chicken breasts in a shallow roasting tin and set aside.

2 Heat the oil in a small pan, and fry the spring onions and garlic for 2 minutes until softenend. Add the honey, orange juice, orange segments and soy sauce to the pan, stirring well until the honey has dissolved.

3 Pour over the chicken and bake, uncovered, for about 45 minutes, basting once or twice until the chicken is cooked. Garnish with lemon balm or parsley and serve the chicken and its sauce with baked potatoes and a salad.

COOK'S TIP

Look out for mustard flavoured with honey to add to this dish instead of the clear honey.

Thai Chicken and Vegetable Stir-Fry

INGREDIENTS

Serves 4

1 piece lemon grass (or the rind of ½ lemon), cut in thin slices
1cm/½in piece of fresh root ginger, chopped
1 large garlic clove, chopped
30ml/2 tbsp sunflower oil
275g/10oz lean chicken, thinly sliced
½ red pepper, seeded and sliced
½ green pepper, seeded and sliced
4 spring onions, chopped
2 medium carrots, cut into matchsticks
115g/4oz fine green beans
30ml/2 tbsp oyster sauce
pinch sugar
salt and black pepper
25g/1oz salted peanuts, lightly crushed, and coriander leaves, to garnish

1 Thinly slice the lemon grass or lemon rind. Peel and chop the ginger and garlic. Heat the oil in a frying pan over a high heat. Add the lemon grass or lemon rind, ginger and garlic, and stir fry for 30 seconds until brown.

2 Add the chicken and stir-fry for 2 minutes. Then add the vegetables and stir-fry for 4–5 minutes, until the chicken is cooked and the vegetables are almost cooked.

3 Finally stir in the oyster sauce, sugar and seasoning to taste and stir-fry for another minute to mix and blend well. Serve at once, sprinkled with the peanuts and coriander leaves and accompanied with rice.

—— COOK'S TIP ——

Make this quick supper dish a little hotter by adding more fresh root ginger, if you wish.

Pasta with Turkey and Tomatoes

INGREDIENTS

Serves 4

675g/1½lb ripe but firm plum
  tomatoes, quartered
90ml/6 tbsp olive oil
5ml/1 tsp dried oregano
350g/12oz broccoli florets
1 small onion, sliced
5ml/1 tsp dried thyme
450g/1lb turkey breast fillets, cubed
3 garlic cloves, finely chopped
15ml/1 tbsp fresh lemon juice
350g/12oz dried pasta twists
salt and black pepper

1 Prehat the oven to 200°C/400°F/
Gas 6. Place the tomatoes in a
baking dish. Drizzle over 15ml/1 tbsp
of the oil, scatter over the oregano and
season with salt.

2 Bake for 30–40 minutes, until the
tomatoes are just browned.

3 Meanwhile, bring a large pan of
salted water to the boil. Add the
broccoli and cook for about 5 minutes,
until just tender. Drain the broccoli
and set aside. Alternatively, steam the
broccoli until tender.

COOK'S TIP

Plum tomatoes are perfect for this dish
but if they are unavailable use any well-
flavoured, firm, yet ripe variety – even
tiny cherry tomatoes.

4 Heat 30ml/2 tbsp of the remaining
oil in a large non-stick frying pan.
Add the onion, thyme, turkey and salt,
to taste. Cook over a high heat for 5–7
minutes, stirring frequently, until the
meat is cooked and beginning to
brown. Add the garlic and cook for a
further 1 minute, stirring frequently.

5 Remove from the heat. Stir in
the lemon juice and season with
pepper. Set aside and keep warm.

6 Bring another large pan of salted
water to the boil. Add the pasta
and cook for 10–12 minutes, until just
tender. Drain and place in a large
serving bowl. Toss the pasta with the
remaining oil.

7 Add the broccoli to the turkey
mixture and toss into the pasta.
Peel the tomatoes and stir gently into
the pasta mixture. Serve immediately.

Chicken with Honey and Grapefruit

Chicken breast portions cook very quickly and are ideal for suppers 'on-the-run' – but don't be tempted to overcook them. You could substitute boneless turkey steaks, or duck breast fillets for the chicken, if you like.

INGREDIENTS

Serves 4
4 chicken breast portions, skinned
45–60ml/3–4 tbsp clear honey
1 pink grapefruit, skinned and cut into
    12 segments
salt and black pepper
three-coloured noodles and salad
    leaves, to serve

1 Make three quite deep, diagonal slits in the chicken flesh using a large sharp knife.

2 Brush the chicken with honey all over and sprinkle with seasoning.

3 Place the chicken in a flameproof dish, uncut side uppermost, under a medium grill for 2–3 minutes, then turn over and place the grapefruit segments in the slits. Brush with more honey and cook for 5 minutes, or until tender.

4 If necessary, reduce the heat so that the honey glazed parts don't burn. Serve at once with three-coloured noodles and salad leaves.

Crispy Chicken with Garlicky Rice

Chicken wings cooked until they are really tender have a surprising amount of meat on them, and make a very economical supper for a crowd of youngsters – provide lots of kitchen paper or napkins for the sticky fingers.

INGREDIENTS

Serves 4
1 large onion, chopped
2 garlic cloves, crushed
30ml/2 tbsp sunflower oil
175g/6oz/⅞ cup patna or basmati rice
350ml/12fl oz/1½ cups hot chicken
    stock
10ml/2 tsp finely grated lemon rind
30ml/2 tbsp chopped mixed herbs
8 or 12 chicken wings
50g/2oz/½ cup plain flour
salt and black pepper

1 Preheat the oven to 200°C/400°F/ Gas 6. Fry the onion and garlic in the oil in a large ovenproof pan until golden. Add the rice and toss until well coated in oil.

2 Stir in the stock, lemon rind and herbs and bring to the boil. Cover and cook in the middle of the oven for 40–50 minutes. Stir the rice once or twice during cooking.

3 Meanwhile, wipe dry the chicken wings. Season the flour and use to coat the chicken portions thoroughly, dusting off any excess.

4 Place the chicken wings in a small roasting tin and cook in the top of the oven for 30–40 minutes, turning once, until crispy and golden.

5 Serve the rice and the crispy chicken wings together with a fresh tomato sauce and a selection of vegetables.

Turkey Spirals

These little spirals may look difficult, but they're very simple to make, and a very good way to pep up plain turkey.

INGREDIENTS

Serves 4

4 thinly sliced turkey breasts, about 90g/3½oz each
20ml/4 tsp tomato purée
15g/½oz/½ cup large basil leaves
1 garlic clove, crushed
15ml/1 tbsp skimmed milk
30ml/2 tbsp wholemeal flour
salt and black pepper
fresh tomato sauce and pasta with fresh basil, to serve

1 Place the turkey steaks on a board. If too thick, flatten them slightly by beating with a rolling pin.

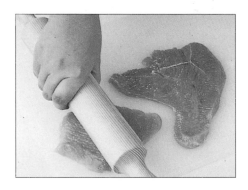

2 Spread each turkey breast with tomato purée, then top with a few leaves of basil, a little crushed garlic, and salt and pepper.

3 Roll up firmly around the filling and secure with a cocktail stick. Brush with milk and sprinkle with flour to coat lightly.

4 Place the spirals on a foil-lined grill pan. Cook under a grill for 15–20 minutes, turning them occasionally, until thoroughly cooked. Serve hot, sliced with a spoonful or two of fresh tomato sauce and pasta, sprinkled with fresh basil.

COOK'S TIP

When flattening the turkey breasts with a rolling pin, place them between two sheets of cling film. Tap them gently and evenly so the meat thins, but doesn't break.

Caribbean Chicken Kebabs

These kebabs have a rich, sunshine Caribbean flavour and the marinade keeps them moist without the need for oil. Serve with a colourful salad and rice.

INGREDIENTS 🍎

Serves 4

500g/1¼lb boneless chicken breasts, skinned
finely grated rind of 1 lime
30ml/2 tbsp lime juice
15ml/1 tbsp rum or sherry
15ml/1 tbsp brown sugar
15ml/1 tsp ground cinnamon
2 mangoes, peeled and cubed
rice and salad, to serve

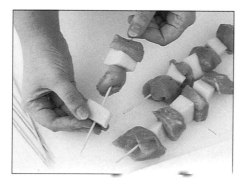

1 Cut the chicken into bite-sized chunks and place in a bowl with the lime rind and juice, rum, sugar, and cinnamon. Toss well, cover, and leave to marinate for 1 hour.

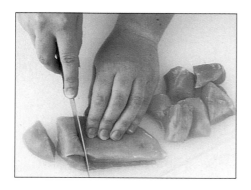

2 Save the juices and thread the chicken onto four wooden skewers, alternating with the mango cubes.

3 Cook the skewers under a grill, or on a barbecue, for 8–10 minutes, turning occasionally and basting with the juices, until the chicken is tender and golden brown. Serve the kebabs at once, with rice and salad.

— COOK'S TIP —

The rum or sherry adds a lovely rich flavour to the marinade, but it is optional so can be omitted if you prefer to avoid the added alcohol.

— VARIATIONS —

Try other fruits in place of the mangoes. Chunks of fresh pineapple or firm peaches or nectarines would be equally good in this recipe.

Chicken with White Wine and Olives

INGREDIENTS

Serves 4

1.5kg/3½lb chicken, cut into pieces
1 onion, sliced
3–6 garlic cloves, finely chopped
5ml/1 tsp dried thyme
475ml/16fl oz/2 cups dry white wine
16–18 stoned green olives
1 bay leaf
15ml/1 tbsp fresh lemon juice
15–25g/½ –1oz/1–2 tbsp butter
black pepper
fresh bay leaves and lemon rind,
  to garnish

1 Heat a large, heavy-based frying pan. When hot, add the chicken pieces, skin-side down, and cook over a medium heat for about 10 minutes, until browned. Turn over the chicken pieces and brown the other side for 5–8 minutes more.

2 Transfer the chicken pieces to a platter and set aside.

3 Drain the excess fat from the pan, leaving about 15ml/1 tbsp. Add the sliced onion and 2.5ml/½ tsp salt and cook for about 5 minutes, until just soft. Add the garlic and thyme and cook for a further 1 minute.

4 Add the wine and stir, scraping up any bits that cling to the pan. Bring to the boil and boil for about 1 minute, then stir in the green olives.

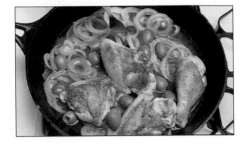

5 Return the chicken pieces to the pan. Add the bay leaf and season lightly with pepper. Reduce the heat, cover and simmer for 20–30 minutes, until the chicken is cooked through.

6 Transfer the chicken pieces to a warm serving dish. Stir the lemon juice into the sauce and whisk in the butter to thicken the sauce slightly. Spoon the sauce over the chicken and serve at once, garnished with bay leaves and lemon rind.

Turkey Meat Loaf

INGREDIENTS

Serves 4

15ml/1 tbsp olive oil
1 onion, chopped
1 green pepper, seeded and finely
  chopped
1 garlic clove, finely chopped
450g/1lb minced turkey
50g/2oz/1 cup fresh white
  breadcrumbs
1 egg, beaten
50g/2oz/½ cup pine nuts
12 sun-dried tomatoes in oil, drained
  and chopped
85ml/3fl oz/⅓ cup milk
10ml/2 tsp chopped fresh rosemary or
  2.5ml/½ tsp dried
5ml/1 tsp fennel seeds
2.5ml/½ tsp dried oregano
salt and black pepper

1 Preheat the oven to 190°C/375°F/ Gas 5. Heat the oil in a frying pan. Add the onion, green pepper and garlic and cook over a low heat for 8–10 minutes, stirring frequently, until the vegetables are just softened. Remove from the heat and leave to cool.

2 Place the minced turkey in a large bowl. Add the onion mixture and all the remaining ingredients and mix together thoroughly.

3 Transfer to a 21 x 11cm/8½ x 4½in loaf tin, packing down firmly. Bake for about 1 hour, until golden brown. Serve with a salad.

Mandarin Sesame Duck

Duck is a high-fat meat but it is possible to get rid of a good proportion of the fat cooked in this way. (If you remove the skin completely, the meat can be dry.) For a special occasion, duck breasts are a good choice, but they are more expensive.

INGREDIENTS 🍎

Serves 4

4 duck legs or boneless breasts
30ml/2 tbsp light soy sauce
45ml/3 tbsp clear honey
15ml/1 tbsp sesame seeds
4 mandarin oranges
5ml/1 tsp cornflour
salt and black pepper

1 Preheat the oven to 180°C/350°F/ Gas 4. Prick the duck skin all over. Slash the breast skin diagonally at intervals with a sharp knife.

2 Place the duck on a rack in a roasting pan and roast for 1 hour. Mix 15ml/1 tbsp soy sauce with 30ml/ 2 tbsp honey and brush over the duck. Sprinkle with sesame seeds. Roast for 15–20 minutes, until golden brown.

3 Meanwhile, grate the rind from one mandarin and squeeze the juice from two. Mix in the cornflour, then stir in the remaining soy sauce and honey. Heat, stirring, until thickened and clear. Season. Peel and slice the remaining mandarins. Serve the duck, with the mandarin slices and the sauce.

— COOK'S TIP —

Use tangerines or clementines, or 1-2 large oranges in place of the mandarins, if you prefer.

Minted Yogurt Chicken

INGREDIENTS 🍎

Serves 4

8 chicken thighs, skinned
15ml/1 tbsp clear honey
30ml/2 tbsp lime or lemon juice
30ml/2 tbsp natural yogurt
60ml/4 tbsp chopped fresh mint
salt and black pepper

1 Slash the chicken flesh at intervals with a sharp knife. Place in a bowl.

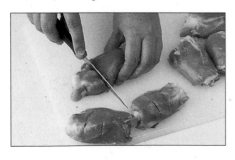

2 Mix the honey, lime or lemon juice, yogurt, seasoning and half the mint.

3 Spoon the marinade over the chicken and leave to marinate for about 30 minutes. Line a grill pan with foil and cook the chicken under a grill until thoroughly cooked and golden brown, turning the chicken occasionally during cooking.

4 Sprinkle with the remaining chopped mint. Serve with potatoes and tomato salad.

— VARIATION —

To make Herby Yogurt Chicken, substitute 60ml/4 tbsp chopped herbs, such as parsley, thyme or chives.

Oven-fried Chicken

INGREDIENTS

Serves 4

4 large chicken portions
50g/2oz/½ cup plain flour
2.5ml/½ tsp salt
1.25ml/¼ tsp black pepper
1 egg
30ml/2 tbsp water
30ml/2 tbsp finely chopped mixed
   fresh herbs, such as parsley, basil, and
   thyme
115g/4oz/1 cup dried white
   breadcrumbs
25g/1oz/¼ cup freshly grated
   Parmesan cheese
lemon wedges, to serve

1 Preheat the oven to 200°C/400°F/ Gas 6. Rinse the chicken portions and pat dry with kitchen paper.

2 Combine the flour, salt and pepper on a large plate and stir with a fork to mix. Coat the chicken portions on all sides with the seasoned flour and shake off the excess.

3 Sprinkle a little water on to the chicken portions and coat again lightly with the seasoned flour.

4 Beat the egg with the water in a shallow dish and stir in the herbs. Dip the chicken portions into the egg mixture, turning to coat them evenly.

5 Combine the breadcrumbs and grated Parmesan cheese on a plate. Roll the chicken portions in the breadcrumbs, patting them in with your fingertips to help them stick.

6 Place the chicken portions in a greased shallow tin large enough to hold them in one layer. Bake for 20–30 minutes, until thoroughly cooked and golden brown. To test whether they are cooked, prick with a fork: the juices that run out should be clear, not pink. Serve at once with lemon wedges.

Chicken in Creamy Orange Sauce

This sauce is deceptively creamy –
in fact it is made with low fat
fromage frais, which is virtually fat-
free. The brandy adds a richer
flavour, but is optional – omit it if
you prefer and use orange juice alone.

INGREDIENTS 🍎

Serves 4

8 chicken thighs or drumsticks,
   skinned
45ml/3 tbsp brandy
300ml/½ pint/1¼ cups orange juice
3 spring onions, chopped
2 tsp cornflour
90ml/6 tbsp low fat fromage frais
salt and black pepper

1 Cook the chicken pieces without
   fat in a non-stick or heavy-based
pan, turning until evenly browned.

2 Stir in the brandy, orange juice and
   spring onions. Bring to a boil, then
cover and simmer for 15 minutes, or
until the chicken is tender and the juices
run clear, not pink, when pierced.

3 Blend the cornflour with a little
   water then mix into the fromage
frais. Stir this into the sauce and stir
over moderate heat until boiling.

4 Adjust the seasoning and serve with
   boiled rice or pasta and green salad.

---- COOK'S TIP ----

Cornflour stabilizes the fromage frais and
helps prevent it curdling

---- VARIATIONS ----

To make Turkey in Creamy Orange
Sauce, substitute 4 turkey steaks for the
chicken thighs or drumsticks.

Chicken with Lemon and Herbs

The herbs can be changed according to what is available; for example, parsley or thyme could be used instead of tarragon and fennel.

INGREDIENTS

Serves 2

50g/2oz/4 tbsp butter
2 spring onions, white part only, finely
   chopped
15ml/1 tbsp chopped fresh tarragon
15ml/1 tbsp chopped fresh fennel
juice of 1 lemon
4 chicken thighs
salt and black pepper
lemon slices and herb sprigs, to garnish

1 Preheat the grill to moderate. In a small saucepan, melt the butter, then add the spring onions, herbs, lemon juice and seasoning.

2 Brush the chicken thighs generously with the herb mixture, then grill for 10–12 minutes, basting frequently with the herb mixture.

3 Turn over the chicken thighs and baste again, then cook for a further 10–12 minutes or until the chicken is cooked and the juices run clear.

4 Serve the chicken garnished with lemon slices and herb sprigs, and accompanied by any remaining herb mixture.

Chicken with Red Cabbage

INGREDIENTS

Serves 4

50g/2oz/4 tbsp butter
4 large chicken portions, halved
1 onion, chopped
500g/1¼lb red cabbage, finely shredded
4 juniper berries, crushed
12 cooked chestnuts
120ml/4fl oz/½ cup full-bodied red
   wine
salt and black pepper

1 Heat the butter in a heavy flame-proof casserole and lightly brown the chicken pieces. Transfer to a plate.

2 Add the onion to the casserole and fry gently until soft and light golden brown. Stir the cabbage and juniper berries into the casserole, season and cook over a moderate heat for 6–7 minutes, stirring once or twice.

3 Stir the chestnuts into the casserole, then tuck the chicken pieces under the cabbage so they are on the bottom of the casserole. Pour in the red wine.

4 Cover and cook gently for about 40 minutes until the chicken juices run clear and the cabbage is very tender. Check the seasoning and serve.

Tandoori Chicken Kebabs

This dish originates from the plains of the Punjab at the foot of the Himalayas. There food is traditionally cooked in clay ovens known as tandoors – hence the name.

INGREDIENTS

Serves 4

4 boneless, skinless chicken breasts
   (about 175g/6oz each)
15ml/1 tbsp lemon juice
45ml/3 tbsp tandoori paste
45ml/3 tbsp natural yogurt
1 garlic clove, crushed
30ml/2 tbsp chopped fresh coriander
1 small onion, cut into wedges and
   separated into layers
a little oil, for brushing
salt and black pepper
fresh coriander sprigs, to garnish
pilau rice and naan bread, to serve

1 Chop the chicken breasts into 2.5cm/1in cubes, place in a bowl and add the lemon juice, tandoori paste, yogurt, garlic, coriander and seasoning. Cover and leave to marinate in the fridge for 2–3 hours.

2 Preheat the grill. Thread alternate pieces of marinated chicken and onion on to four skewers.

3 Brush the onions with a little oil, lay on a grill rack and cook under a high heat for 10–12 minutes, turning once. Garnish the kebabs with fresh coriander and serve at once with pilau rice and naan bread.

--- COOK'S TIP ---

Use chopped, boned and skinless chicken thighs, or turkey breasts for a cheaper alternative.

Chinese Chicken with Cashew Nuts

INGREDIENTS

Serves 4

4 boneless chicken breasts (about
   175g/6oz each), skinned and sliced
   into strips
3 garlic cloves, crushed
60ml/4 tbsp soy sauce
30ml/2 tbsp cornflour
225g/8oz dried egg noodles
45ml/3 tbsp groundnut or sunflower oil
15ml/1 tbsp sesame oil
115g/4oz/1 cup roasted cashew nuts
6 spring onions, cut into 5cm/2in
   pieces and halved lengthways
spring onion curls and a little chopped
   red chilli, to garnish

1 Place the chicken in a bowl with the garlic, soy sauce and cornflour and mix until the chicken is well coated. Cover and chill for about 30 minutes.

2 Meanwhile, bring a pan of water to the boil and add the egg noodles. Turn off the heat and leave to stand for 5 minutes. Drain well and reserve.

3 Heat the oils in a large frying pan or wok and add the chilled chicken and marinade juices. Stir-fry on a high heat for about 3–4 minutes, or until golden brown.

4 Add the cashew nuts and spring onions to the pan or wok and stir-fry for 2–3 minutes.

5 Add the drained noodles and stir-fry for a further 2 minutes. Toss the noodles well and serve immediately, garnished with the spring onion curls and chopped chilli.

Hampshire Farmhouse Flan

INGREDIENTS

Serves 4

225g/8oz/2 cups wholemeal flour
50g/2oz/4 tbsp butter, cubed
50g/2oz/4 tbsp lard
5ml/1 tsp caraway seeds
15ml/1 tbsp oil
1 onion, chopped
1 garlic clove, crushed
225g/8oz/2 cups chopped cooked
  chicken
75g/3oz/2½ cups watercress leaves,
  chopped
grated rind of ½ small lemon
2 eggs, lightly beaten
175ml/6fl oz/¾ cup double cream
45ml/3 tbsp natural yogurt
a good pinch of grated nutmeg
45ml/3 tbsp grated Caerphilly cheese
beaten egg, to glaze
salt and black pepper

1 Place the flour in a bowl with a pinch of salt. Add the butter and lard and rub into the flour with your fingertips until the mixture resembles breadcrumbs. (Alternatively, you can use a food processor.)

2 Stir in the caraway seeds and 45ml/3 tbsp iced water and mix to a firm dough. Knead lightly on a floured surface until smooth.

3 Roll out the pastry and use to line an 18 x 28cm/7 x 11in loose-based flan tin. Reserve the trimmings. Prick the base and chill for 20 minutes. Place a baking sheet in the oven and preheat to 200°C/400°F/Gas 6.

4 Heat the oil in a frying pan and sauté the onions and garlic for 5–6 minutes, until just softened. Remove from the heat and cool.

5 Line the pastry case with grease-proof paper and fill with baking beans. Bake for 10 minutes, then remove the paper and beans and cook for 5 minutes.

6 Mix together the onions, chicken, watercress and lemon rind and spoon into the flan case. Beat the eggs, cream, yogurt, nutmeg, cheese and seasoning and pour over the chicken mix.

7 Roll out the pastry trimmings and cut out 1cm/½in strips. Brush with egg, then twist each strip and lay in a lattice over the flan. Press the ends on to the pastry edge. Bake for about 35 minutes, until the top is golden.

Chicken Biryani

INGREDIENTS

Serves 4

275g/10oz/1½ cups basmati rice, rinsed
2.5ml/½ tsp salt
5 whole cardamom pods
2–3 whole cloves
1 cinnamon stick
45ml/3 tbsp vegetable oil
3 onions, sliced
675g/1½lb boneless, skinned chicken
  (4 x 175g/6oz chicken breasts),
  cubed
1.25ml/¼ tsp ground cloves
5 cardamom pods, seeds removed and
  ground
1.25ml/¼ tsp hot chilli powder
5ml/1 tsp ground cumin
5ml/1 tsp ground coriander
2.5ml/½ tsp freshly ground black
  pepper
3 garlic cloves, finely chopped
5ml/1 tsp finely chopped fresh root
  ginger
juice of 1 lemon
4 tomatoes, sliced
30ml/2 tbsp chopped fresh coriander
150ml/5fl oz/⅔ cup natural yogurt
2.5ml/½ tsp saffron strands soaked in
  10ml/2 tsp hot milk
45ml/3 tbsp toasted flaked almonds
  and fresh coriander sprigs, to garnish
natural yogurt, to serve

1 Preheat the oven to 190°C/375°F/ Gas 5. Bring a pan of water to the boil and add the rice, salt, cardamom pods, cloves and cinnamon stick. Boil for 2 minutes and then drain, leaving the whole spices in the rice.

2 Heat the oil in a pan and fry the onions for 8 minutes, until browned. Add the chicken followed by all the ground spices, the garlic, ginger and lemon juice. Stir-fry for 5 minutes.

3 Transfer the chicken mixture to an ovenproof casserole and lay the tomatoes on top. Sprinkle over the fresh coriander, spoon over the yogurt and top with the drained rice.

4 Drizzle the saffron and milk over the rice and pour over about 150ml/¼ pint/⅔ cup of water.

5 Cover tightly and bake in the oven for 1 hour. Transfer to a warmed serving platter and remove the whole spices from the rice. Garnish with toasted almonds and fresh coriander and serve with yogurt.

DINNER PARTY DISHES

Chicken, duck, turkey and game dishes are ideal if you are entertaining – not too expensive, generally light to eat and, on the whole, quick and easy to prepare. There are dishes here suitable for special occasions and celebrations, such as Venison with Cranberry Sauce, or Turkey with Yellow Pepper Sauce, and other simpler, yet equally delicious recipes for unexpected guests, such as Duck Breasts with Orange.

Normandy Roast Chicken

INGREDIENTS

Serves 4

50g/2oz/4 tbsp butter, softened
30ml/2 tbsp chopped fresh tarragon
1 small garlic clove, crushed
1.5kg/3lb fresh chicken
5ml/1 tsp plain flour
150ml/¼ pint/⅔ cup single cream or
    crème fraîche
a good squeeze of lemon juice
salt and black pepper
fresh tarragon and lemon slices,
    to garnish

1 Preheat the oven to 200°C/400°F/
Gas 6. Mix together the butter,
15ml/1 tbsp of the chopped tarragon,
the garlic and seasoning in a bowl.
Spoon half the butter into the cavity of
the chicken.

2 Carefully lift the skin at the neck
end of the bird away from the
breast flesh on each side, then gently
push a little of the butter into each
pocket and smooth down over the
breast with your fingers.

3 Season the bird and lay it, breast
down, in a roasting tin. Roast in
the oven for 45 minutes, then turn the
chicken over and baste with the juices.
Cook for a further 45 minutes.

4 When the chicken is cooked, lift it
to drain out any juices from the
cavity into the tin, then transfer the
bird to a warmed platter.

5 Place the roasting tin on the hob
and heat until sizzling. Stir in the
flour and cook for 1 minute, then stir
in the cream, the remaining tarragon,
150ml/¼ pint/⅔ cup water, the lemon
juice and seasoning. Boil and stir for
2–3 minutes, until thickened. Garnish
the chicken with tarragon and lemon
slices and serve with the sauce.

Duck Breasts with Orange Sauce

A simple variation on the classic
French whole roast duck.

INGREDIENTS

Serves 4

4 duck breasts
15ml/1 tbsp sunflower oil
2 oranges
150ml/¼ pint/⅔ cup fresh orange juice
15ml/1 tbsp port
30ml/2 tbsp Seville orange marmalade
15g/½oz/1 tbsp butter
5ml/1 tsp cornflour
salt and black pepper

1 Season the duck breast skin. Heat
the oil in a frying pan over a moderate heat and add the duck breasts, skin
side down. Cover and cook for 3–4
minutes, until lightly browned. Turn
the breasts over, lower the heat slightly
and cook uncovered for 5–6 minutes.

2 Peel the skin and pith from the
oranges. Working over a bowl to
catch any juice, slice either side of the
membranes to release the orange
segments, then set aside with the juice.

3 Remove the duck breasts from the
pan with a slotted spoon, drain on
kitchen paper and keep warm in the
oven while making the sauce. Drain off
the fat from the pan.

4 Add the segmented oranges, all but
30ml/2 tbsp of the orange juice, the
port and the orange marmalade to the
pan. Bring to the boil and then reduce
the heat slightly. Whisk small knobs of
the butter into the sauce and season.

5 Blend the cornflour with the
reserved orange juice, pour into the
pan and stir until slightly thickened. Add
the duck breasts and cook gently for
about 3 minutes. To serve, arrange the
sliced breasts on plates with the sauce.

Venison with Cranberry Sauce

Venison steaks are now readily available. Lean and low in fat, they make a healthy choice for a special occasion. Served with a sauce of fresh seasonal cranberries, port and ginger, they make a dish with a wonderful combination of flavours.

INGREDIENTS

Serves 4

1 orange
1 lemon
75g/3oz/1 cup fresh or frozen
  cranberries
5ml/1 tsp grated fresh root ginger
1 thyme sprig
5ml/1 tsp Dijon mustard
60ml/4 tbsp redcurrant jelly
150ml/¼ pint/⅔ cup ruby port
30ml/2 tbsp sunflower oil
4 venison steaks
2 shallots, finely chopped
salt and black pepper
thyme sprigs, to garnish
creamy mashed potatoes and broccoli,
  to serve

1 Pare the rind from half the orange and half the lemon using a vegetable peeler, then cut into very fine strips.

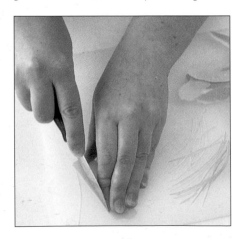

2 Blanch the strips in a small pan of boiling water for about 5 minutes until tender. Drain the strips and refresh under cold water.

3 Squeeze the juice from the orange and lemon and then pour into a small pan. Add the fresh or frozen cranberries, ginger, thyme sprig, mustard, redcurrant jelly and port. Cook over a low heat until the jelly melts.

4 Bring the sauce to the boil, stirring occasionally, then cover the pan and reduce the heat. Cook gently, for about 15 minutes, until the cranberries are just tender.

5 Heat the oil in a heavy-based frying pan, add the venison steaks and cook over a high heat for 2–3 minutes.

6 Turn over the steaks and add the shallots to the pan. Cook the steaks on the other side for 2–3 minutes, depending on whether you like rare or medium cooked meat.

7 Just before the end of cooking, pour in the sauce and add the strips of orange and lemon rind.

8 Leave the sauce to bubble for a few seconds to thicken slightly, then remove the thyme sprig and adjust the seasoning to taste.

9 Transfer the venison steaks to warmed plates and spoon over the sauce. Garnish with thyme sprigs and serve accompanied by creamy mashed potatoes and broccoli.

COOK'S TIP

When frying venison, always remember the briefer the better; venison will turn to leather if subjected to fierce heat after it has reached the medium-rare stage. If you dislike any hint of pink, cook it to this stage then let it rest in a low oven for a few minutes.

VARIATION

When fresh cranberries are unavailable, use redcurrants instead. Stir them into the sauce towards the end of cooking with the orange and lemon rinds.

Rabbit with Parsley Sauce

INGREDIENTS

Serves 4

90ml/6 tbsp soy sauce
few drops of Tabasco sauce
5ml/1 tbsp sweet paprika
5ml/1 tbsp dried basil
1–1.5kg/2–3lb rabbit, cut into pieces
45ml/3 tbsp peanut or olive oil
75g/3oz/¾ cup plain flour
1 large onion, finely sliced
250ml/8fl oz/1 cup dry white wine
250ml/8fl oz/1 cup chicken stock
2 cloves garlic, finely chopped
60ml/4 tbsp fresh chopped parsley
salt and white pepper
mashed potatoes or rice, to serve
fresh parsley sprigs, to garnish

1 Combine the soy sauce, Tabasco sauce, white pepper, paprika, and basil in a medium-sized bowl. Add the rabbit pieces and turn them over in the mixture so they are coated thoroughly. Leave to marinate for at least 1 hour.

2 Heat the oil in a flameproof casserole. Coat the rabbit pieces lightly in the flour, shaking off the excess. Brown the rabbit pieces in the hot oil for about 5–6 minutes, turning them frequently. Remove the rabbit pieces with a slotted spoon and set aside on a plate or dish. Preheat the oven to 180°C/350°F/Gas 4.

3 Add the onion to the casserole and cook over a low heat for 8–10 minutes, until softened. Increase the heat, add the wine, and stir well to mix in all the cooking juices.

4 Return the rabbit and any juices to the casserole. Add the stock, garlic, parsley and salt. Mix well and turn the rabbit to coat with the sauce. Cover and place in the oven. Cook for about 1 hour, until the rabbit is tender, stirring occasionally. Serve garnished with parsley sprigs and accompanied by mashed potatoes or rice.

Cajun-spiced Chicken

INGREDIENTS

Serves 6

6 medium skinless boneless chicken
   breasts
75g/3oz/6 tbsp butter or margarine
5ml/1 tsp garlic powder
10ml/2 tsp onion powder
5ml/2 tsp cayenne pepper
10ml/2 tsp paprika
7.5ml/1½ tsp salt
2.5ml/½ tsp white pepper
5ml/1 tsp black pepper
1.25ml/¼ tsp ground cumin
5ml/1 tsp dried thyme
salad leaves and pepper strips,
   to garnish

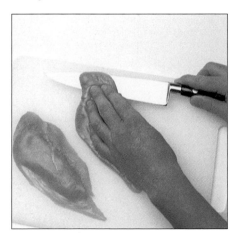

1 Slice each chicken breast in half
horizontally, making two pieces of
about the same thickness. Flatten them
slightly with the heel of your hand.

2 Melt the butter or margarine in a
small saucepan over a low heat.

3 Combine all the remaining
ingredients in a bowl and stir to
blend well. Brush the chicken pieces
on both sides with a little of the melted
butter or margarine, then sprinkle
evenly with the seasoning mixture.

4 Heat a large heavy-based frying
pan over high heat for about
5–8 minutes, until a drop of water
sprinkled on the surface sizzles.

5 Drizzle 5ml/1 tsp melted butter on
to each chicken piece. Place them
in the frying pan in an even layer, two
or three at a time, and cook for 2–3
minutes, until the underside begins to
blacken. Turn and cook the other side
for 2–3 minutes more. Serve hot with
salad leaves and pepper strips

VARIATION

For Cajun-spiced Fish substitute six white
fish fillets for the chicken. Do not slice the
fish fillets in half, but season as for the
chicken and cook for 2 minutes on one
side and 1½–2 minutes on the other, until
the fish flakes easily.

Lemon Chicken with Guacamole Sauce

INGREDIENTS

Serves 4

juice of 2 lemons
45ml/3 tbsp olive oil
2 garlic cloves, finely chopped
4 chicken breasts, about 200g/7oz each
2 large tomatoes, cored and cut in half
salt and black pepper
chopped fresh coriander, to garnish

For the sauce

1 ripe avocado
60ml/4 tbsp soured cream
45ml/3 tbsp fresh lemon juice
2.5ml/½ tsp salt
50ml/2fl oz/¼ cup water

1 Combine the lemon juice, oil, garlic, 2.5ml/½ tsp salt and a little pepper in a bowl. Stir to mix.

VARIATION

To barbecue the chicken, prepare the fire, and when the coals are glowing red and covered with grey ash, spread them in a single layer. Set an oiled rack about 13cm/5in above the coals and cook the chicken breasts for about 15–20 minutes until lightly charred and cooked through, brushing with oil, to baste.

2 Arrange the chicken breasts, in one layer, in a shallow glass or ceramic dish. Pour over the lemon mixture and turn to coat evenly. Cover and leave to stand for at least 1 hour at room temperature, or chill overnight.

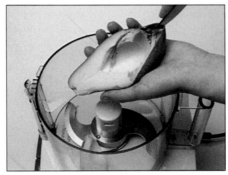

3 To make the sauce, halve the avocado, remove the stone and scrape the flesh into a food processor.

4 Add the soured cream, lemon juice and salt and process until smooth. Add the water and process just to blend. If necessary, add a little more water to thin the sauce. Transfer to a bowl, taste and adjust the seasoning if necessary. Set aside in a cool place.

5 Preheat the grill and heat a ridged frying pan. Remove the chicken from the marinade and pat dry.

6 When the frying pan is hot, add the chicken breasts and cook for about 10 minutes, turning them frequently, until they are cooked through.

7 Meanwhile, arrange the tomato halves, cut-sides up, on a baking sheet and season lightly with salt and black pepper. Grill for about 5 minutes, until hot and bubbling.

8 To serve, place a chicken breast, tomato half and a dollop of avocado sauce on each plate. Sprinkle with chopped coriander and serve.

Pheasant with Apples

Pheasant is worth buying as it is low in fat, full of flavour, and never dry when cooked like this.

INGREDIENTS 🍎

Serves 4
1 pheasant
2 small onions, quartered
3 celery stalks, thickly sliced
2 red eating apples, thickly sliced
120ml/4fl oz/½ cup stock
15ml/1 tbsp clear honey
30ml/2 tbsp Worcestershire sauce
ground nutmeg
2 tbsp toasted hazelnuts
salt and black pepper

1 Preheat the oven to 180°C/350°F/ Gas 4. Sauté the pheasant without fat in a non-stick pan, turning occasionally until golden. Remove and keep hot.

2 Sauté the onions and celery in the pan to brown lightly. Spoon into a casserole and place the pheasant on top. Tuck the apple slices around it.

3 Spoon over the stock, honey, and Worcestershire sauce. Sprinkle with nutmeg, salt and pepper, cover, and bake for 1¼ –1½ hours or until tender. Sprinkle with nuts and serve hot.

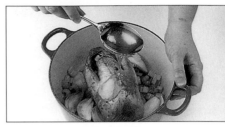

— COOK'S TIP —

Choose a firm variety of eating apple for this recipe, less acidic fruits hold their shape best.

Cider-baked Rabbit

Rabbit is a low fat meat and an economical choice for family meals. Chicken pieces may be used as an alternative.

INGREDIENTS 🍎

Serves 4
450g/1lb rabbit pieces
15ml/1 tbsp plain flour
5ml/1 tsp dry mustard
3 medium leeks, thickly sliced
250ml/8fl oz/1 cup dry cider
2 sprigs rosemary
salt and black pepper
fresh rosemary, to garnish

1 Preheat the oven to 180°C/350°F/ Gas 4. Place the rabbit pieces in a bowl and sprinkle over the flour and mustard. Toss to coat evenly.

2 Arrange the rabbit in one layer in a wide casserole. Blanch the leeks in boiling water, then drain and add to the casserole.

3 Add the cider, rosemary, and seasoning, cover, then bake for 1–1¼ hours, or until the rabbit is tender. Garnish with fresh rosemary, and serve with baked potatoes and vegetables.

— VARIATION —

To make Cider-baked Chicken, substitute small chicken joints, such as thighs or drumsticks for the rabbit pieces.

Oat-coated Chicken with Sage

Rolled oats make a good coating for savoury foods, and offer a good way to add extra fibre.

INGREDIENTS

Serves 4

45ml/3 tbsp skimmed milk
10ml/2 tsp English mustard
115g/4oz/½ cup rolled oats
45ml/3 tbsp chopped sage leaves
8 chicken thighs or drumsticks,
  skinned
½ cup low fat fromage frais
5ml/1 tsp wholegrain mustard
salt and black pepper
fresh sage leaves, to garnish

1 Preheat the oven to 200°C/400°F/ Gas 6. Mix together the milk and plain mustard.

2 Mix the oats with 30ml/2 tbsp of the sage and the seasoning on a plate. Brush the chicken with the milk and press into the oats to coat.

3 Place the chicken on a baking sheet and bake for about 40 minutes, or until the juices run clear, not pink, when pierced through the thickest part.

4 Meanwhile, mix together the low fat fromage frais, mustard, remaining sage and seasoning, then serve with the chicken. Garnish the chicken with fresh sage and serve hot or cold.

COOK'S TIP

If fresh sage is not available, choose another fresh herb such as thyme or parsley, instead of using a dried alternative.

VARIATION

For the sauce, use natural yogurt or Italian ricotta cheese in place of the fromage frais, if you prefer.

Turkey with Yellow Pepper Sauce

INGREDIENTS

Serves 4

30ml/2 tbsp olive oil
2 large yellow peppers, seeded and
   chopped
1 small onion, chopped
15ml/1 tbsp freshly squeezed orange
   juice
300ml/½ pint/1¼ cups chicken stock
4 turkey escalopes
75g/3oz Boursin or garlicky cream
   cheese
12 fresh basil leaves
25g/1oz/2 tbsp butter
salt and black pepper

1 To make the yellow pepper sauce;
   heat half the oil in a pan and gently
fry the peppers and onion until beginning to soften. Add the orange juice
and stock and cook until very soft.

2 Meanwhile, lay the turkey escalopes
   out flat and beat them out lightly.

3 Spread the turkey escalopes with
   the Boursin or garlicky cream
cheese. Chop half the basil and sprinkle
on top, then roll up, tucking in the
ends like an envelope, and secure neatly with half a cocktail stick.

4 Heat the remaining oil and the
   butter in a frying pan and fry the
escalopes for 7–8 minutes, turning
them frequently, until golden and
cooked.

5 While the escalopes are cooking,
   press the pepper mixture through
a sieve, or blend until smooth, then
strain back into the pan. Season to taste
and warm through, or serve cold, with
the escalopes, garnished with the
remaining basil leaves.

— COOK'S TIP —

Chicken breast fillets or veal escalopes
could be used in place of the turkey, if
you prefer.

Crumbed Turkey Steaks

The authentic Austrian recipe for *Weiner Schnitzel* uses veal escalopes (in fact it originally comes from Milan in Italy, where Parmesan cheese replaced the breadcrumbs). Turkey breasts make a tasty alternative.

INGREDIENTS

Serves 4
4 turkey breast steaks (about
 150g/5oz each)
45ml/3 tbsp plain flour, seasoned
1 egg, lightly beaten
75g/3oz/1½ cups fresh breadcrumbs
25g/1oz/5 tbsp finely grated Parmesan
 cheese
25g/1oz/2 tbsp butter
45ml/3 tbsp sunflower oil
fresh parsley, to garnish
4 lemon wedges, to serve

1 Lay the turkey steaks between two sheets of greaseproof paper. Bash each one with a rolling pin until flattened. Snip the edges of the steaks with scissors a few times to prevent them curling during cooking.

2 Place the seasoned flour on one plate, the egg into another and the breadcrumbs and Parmesan mixed together on a third plate.

3 Dip each side of the steaks into the flour and shake off any excess. Next, dip them into the egg and then gently press each side into the bread-crumbs and cheese until evenly coated.

4 Heat the butter and oil in a large frying pan and fry the turkey steaks on a moderate heat for 2–3 minutes on each side, until golden. Garnish with parsley and serve with lemon wedges.

Country Cider Hot-pot

Rabbit flavoured with cider makes a delicious casserole dish.

INGREDIENTS

Serves 4
30ml/2 tbsp plain flour
4 boneless rabbit portions
25g/1oz/2 tbsp butter
15ml/1 tbsp vegetable oil
15 baby onions
4 rashers streaky bacon, chopped
10ml/2 tsp Dijon mustard
450ml/¾ pint/1⅞ cups dry cider
3 carrots, chopped
2 parsnips, chopped
12 ready-to-eat prunes, stoned
1 fresh rosemary sprig
1 bay leaf
salt and black pepper

1 Preheat the oven to 160°C/325°F/ Gas 3. Place the flour and season-ing in a plastic bag, add the rabbit por-tions and shake until coated. Set aside.

2 Heat the butter and oil in a flame-proof casserole and add the onions and bacon. Fry for 4 minutes, until the onions have softened. Remove with a draining spoon and reserve.

3 Fry the seasoned rabbit portions in the oil in the flameproof casserole until they are browned all over, then spread a little of the mustard over the top of each portion.

4 Return the onions and bacon to the pan. Pour on the cider and add the carrots, parsnips, prunes, rosemary and bay leaf. Season well. Bring to the boil, then cover and transfer to the oven. Cook for about 1½ hours until tender.

5 Remove the rosemary sprig and bay leaf and serve the rabbit hot with creamy mashed potatoes.

Chicken, Pepper and Bean Stew

INGREDIENTS

Serves 4–6

1.75kg/4lb chicken, cut into pieces
paprika
30ml/2 tbsp olive oil
25g/1oz/2 tbsp butter
2 onions, chopped
½ each green and yellow pepper,
   chopped
450g/1lb/2 cups peeled, chopped,
   fresh or canned plum tomatoes
250ml/8fl oz/1 cup white wine
475ml/16fl oz/2 cups chicken stock
   or water
45ml/3 tbsp chopped fresh parsley
2.5ml/½ tbsp Tabasco sauce
15ml/1 tbsp Worcestershire sauce
2 x 200g/7oz cans sweetcorn
115g/4oz broad beans (fresh or frozen)
45ml/3 tbsp plain flour
salt and black pepper
fresh parsley sprigs, to garnish

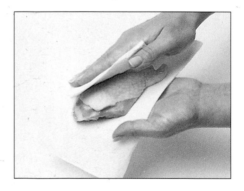

1 Rinse the chicken pieces under cold water and pat dry with kitchen paper. Sprinkle each piece lightly with salt and a little paprika.

2 Heat the olive oil with the butter in a flameproof casserole or large heavy-based saucepan over a medium-high heat, until the mixture is sizzling and just starting to change colour.

3 Add the chicken pieces and fry until golden brown on all sides, cooking in batches, if necessary. Remove from the pan with tongs and set aside.

4 Reduce the heat and add the onions and peppers to the pan. Cook for 8–10 minutes, until softened.

5 Increase the heat. Add the tomatoes and their juice, the wine, stock or water, parsley and Tabasco sauce and Worcestershire sauce. Stir thoroughly and bring to the boil.

6 Add the chicken to the pan, pushing the pieces down into the sauce. Cover, reduce the heat, and simmer for 30 minutes, stirring.

7 Remove the lid, add the sweetcorn and beans and mix well. Partly cover the pan and cook for 30 minutes.

8 Tilt the pan and skim off as much of the surface fat as possible. Mix the flour with a little water in a small bowl to make a paste.

9 Stir in about 175ml/6fl oz/¾ cup of the hot sauce from the pan into the flour mixture and then stir into the stew and mix well. Cook for 5–8 minutes more, stirring occasionally.

10 Check the seasoning and adjust if necessary. Serve the stew in shallow soup dishes or large bowls, garnished with parsley sprigs.

Poussin with Grapes in Vermouth

INGREDIENTS

Serves 4

4 oven-ready poussin, about
  450g/1lb each
50g/2oz/4 tbsp butter, softened
2 shallots, chopped
60ml/4 tbsp chopped fresh parsley
225g/8oz white grapes, preferably
  muscatel, halved and seeded
150ml/¼ pint/⅔ cup white vermouth
5ml/1 tsp cornflour
60ml/4 tbsp double cream
30ml/2 tbsp pine nuts, toasted
salt and black pepper
watercress sprigs, to garnish

1 Preheat the oven to 200°C/400°F/
Gas 6. Wash and dry the poussin.
Spread the softened butter all over the
poussin and put a hazelnut-sized piece
in the cavity of each bird.

2 Mix together the shallots and parsley
and place a quarter of the mixture
inside each poussin. Put the poussin side
by side in a large roasting tin and roast
for 40–50 minutes, or until the juices
run clear when the thickest part of the
flesh is pierced with a skewer. Transfer
the poussin to a warmed serving plate.
Cover and keep warm.

3 Skim off most of the fat from the
roasting tin, then add the grapes
and vermouth. Place the tin directly
over a low flame for a few minutes to
warm and slightly soften the grapes.

4 Lift the grapes out of the tin using a
slotted spoon and scatter them
around the poussin. Keep covered. Stir
the cornflour into the cream, then add
to the pan juices. Cook gently for a few
minutes, stirring, until the sauce has
thickened. Taste and adjust seasoning.

5 Pour the sauce around the poussin.
Sprinkle with the toasted pine nuts
and garnish with watercress sprigs.

Guinea Fowl with Cider and Apples

Guinea fowl are farmed, so they are available quite frequently in supermarkets, usually fresh. Their flavour is reminiscent of an old-fashioned chicken – not really gamey, but they do have slightly darker meat.

INGREDIENTS

Serves 4–6
1.75kg/4–4½lb guinea fowl
1 onion, halved
3 celery sticks
3 bay leaves
little butter
300ml/½ pint/1¼ cups dry cider
150ml/¼ pint/⅔ cup chicken stock
2 small apples, peeled and sliced
60ml/4 tbsp thick double cream
few sage leaves
30ml/2 tbsp chopped fresh parsley
salt and black pepper

1 If the guinea fowl is packed with its giblets, put them in a pan with water to cover, half the onion, a stick of celery, a bay leaf and seasoning. Simmer for 30 minutes, or until you have about 150ml/¼ pint/⅔ cup well-flavoured stock.

2 Preheat the oven to 190°C/375°F/ Gas 5. Wash and wipe dry the bird and place the remaining onion half and a knob of butter inside the body cavity. Place in a roasting dish, sprinkle with seasoning to taste, and dot with a few knobs of butter.

3 Pour the cider and chicken stock into the dish and cover with a lid or foil. Bake for 25 minutes per 450g/ 1lb, basting occasionally.

4 Uncover for the last 20 minutes, baste well again and add the prepared apples and the celery, sliced. When the guinea fowl is cooked, transfer it to a warm serving dish and keep warm. Remove the apples and celery with a slotted spoon and set aside.

5 Boil the liquid rapidly to reduce to about 150ml/¼ pint/⅔ cup. Stir in the cream, seasoning to taste and the sage leaves, and cook for a few minutes more to reduce slightly. Return the apples to this pan with the parsley and warm through, then serve with or around the bird.

Coronation Chicken

INGREDIENTS

Serves 8

½ lemon
2.3kg/5lb chicken
1 onion, quartered
1 carrot, quartered
large bouquet garni
8 black peppercorns, crushed
salt
watercress sprigs, to garnish

For the sauce

1 small onion, chopped
15 g/½ oz/1 tbsp butter
15ml/1 tbsp curry paste
15ml/1 tbsp tomato purée
120ml/4fl oz/½ cup red wine
bay leaf
juice of ½ lemon, or more to taste
10–15ml/2–3 tsp apricot jam
300ml/½ pint/1¼ cups mayonnaise
120ml/4fl oz/½ cup whipping cream,
    whipped
salt and black pepper

1 Put the lemon half in the chicken cavity, then place the chicken in a saucepan that it just fits. Add the vegetables, bouquet garni, peppercorns and salt to the pan.

2 Add sufficient water to come two-thirds of the way up the chicken, bring to the boil, then cover and cook gently for about 1½ hours, until the chicken juices run clear.

3 Transfer the chicken to a large bowl, pour over the cooking liquid and leave to cool. When cold, skin and bone the chicken, then chop.

4 Make the sauce, cook the onion in the butter until soft. Add the curry paste, tomato purée, wine, bay leaf and lemon juice, then cook for 10 minutes. Add the jam, then sieve and cool.

5 Beat into the mayonnaise. Fold in the cream, then add seasoning and lemon juice. Garnish with watercress.

Duck with Cumberland Sauce

INGREDIENTS

Serves 4

4 duck portions
grated rind and juice of 1 lemon
grated rind and juice of 1 large orange
60ml/4 tbsp redcurrant jelly
60ml/4 tbsp port
pinch of ground mace or ginger
15ml/1 tbsp brandy
salt and black pepper
orange slices, to garnish

1 Preheat the oven to 190°C/375°F/ Gas 5. Place a rack in a roasting tin. Prick the duck portions all over, sprinkle with salt and pepper. Place the duck portions on the rack and cook in the oven for 45–50 minutes, until the duck skin is crisp and the juices run clear.

2 Meanwhile, simmer the lemon and orange juices and rinds together in a saucepan for 5 minutes.

3 Stir in the redcurrant jelly until melted, then stir in the port. Bring to the boil, add mace or ginger and seasoning to taste.

4 Transfer the duck to a serving plate; keep warm. Pour the fat from the roasting tin, leaving the cooking juices. With the tin over a low heat, stir in the brandy, dislodging the sediment and bring to the boil. Stir in the port sauce and serve with the duck, garnished with orange slices.

Chicken in Green Sauce

Slow, gentle cooking makes the chicken succulent and tender.

Ingredients

Serves 4

25g/1oz/2 tbsp butter
15ml/1 tbsp olive oil
4 chicken portions
1 small onion, finely chopped
150ml/¼ pint/⅔ cup medium-bodied
  dry white wine
150ml/¼ pint/⅔ cup chicken stock
175g/6oz watercress
2 thyme sprigs and 2 tarragon
  sprigs
150ml/¼ pint/⅔ cup double cream
salt and black pepper
watercress leaves, to garnish

1 Heat the butter and oil in a heavy shallow pan, then brown the chicken evenly. Transfer the chicken to a plate using a slotted spoon and keep warm in the oven.

2 Add the onion to the cooking juices in the pan and cook until softened but not coloured.

3 Stir in the wine, boil for 2–3 minutes, then add the stock and bring to the boil. Return the chicken to the pan, cover tightly and cook very gently for about 30 minutes, until the chicken juices run clear. Then transfer the chicken to a warm dish, cover the dish and keep warm.

4 Boil the cooking juices hard until reduced to about 60ml/4 tbsp. Remove the leaves from the watercress and herbs, add to the pan with the cream and simmer over a medium heat until slightly thickened.

5 Return the chicken to the casserole, season and heat through for a few minutes. Garnish with watercress leaves to serve.

COOK'S TIP

You could use boneless turkey steaks in place of the chicken portions in this recipe, if you prefer.

Tuscan Chicken

This simple peasant casserole has all
the flavours of traditional Tuscan
ingredients. The wine can be
replaced by chicken stock.

INGREDIENTS 🍎

Serves 4

8 chicken thighs, skinned
5ml/1 tsp olive oil
1 medium onion, sliced thinly
2 red peppers, seeded and sliced
1 garlic clove, crushed
300ml/½ pint/1¼ cups puréed
   tomatoes (passata)
150ml/¼ pint/⅔ cup dry white wine
large sprig fresh oregano, or 5ml/1 tsp
   dried oregano
400g/14oz can cannellini beans, drained
45ml/3 tbsp fresh bread crumbs
salt and black pepper

1 Cook the chicken in the oil in a
nonstick or heavy pan until golden
brown. Remove and keep hot. Add the
onion and bell peppers to the pan and
gently sauté until softened, but not
brown. Stir in the garlic.

2 Add the chicken, tomatoes, wine,
and oregano. Season well, bring to
a boil, then cover the pan tightly.

——— COOK'S TIP ———

In the summer, when fresh herbs are
abundant, stir in a handful of fresh
chopped parsley just before sprinkling with
the breadcrumbs.

---

3 Lower the heat and simmer gently,
stirring occasionally for 30–35
minutes or until the chicken is tender
and the juices run clear, not pink,
when pierced with the point of a knife.

4 Stir in the cannellini beans and
simmer for 5 minutes more, until
heated through. Sprinkle with the
bread crumbs and cook under a broiler
until golden brown.

Duck Breasts with Blackberries

If there isn't any blackberry, or bramble, jelly in your store-cupboard, you could substitute redcurrant jelly instead.

INGREDIENTS

Serves 4
4 duck breasts
finely grated rind and juice of 1 orange
30ml/2 tbsp blackberry (bramble) jelly
salt and black pepper

1 Heat a heavy-based frying pan and place the duck portions skin side down first. Fry for 3–4 minutes. Meanwhile, sprinkle the meat side with seasoning and the orange rind.

2 Turn the duck over and continue cooking for 3–4 minutes. Spread the skin side with some of the blackberry jelly while cooking, and pour the orange juice over the portions.

3 Spread a little more jelly over the duck breasts, then turn them over and cook for 1–2 minutes more, until just cooked, but still slightly pink in the middle. Serve the duck breasts with the glaze poured over, accompanied by new potatoes and a watercress and orange salad.

Spring Rabbit Casserole

If you have never tried rabbit before, you will find it very similar to chicken, but with just a slightly sweeter taste. You could replace the rabbit with chicken in this recipe, if you prefer – cook it in exactly the same way.

INGREDIENTS

Serves 4
15ml/1 tbsp sunflower oil
450g/1lb boneless rabbit
4 rashers streaky bacon, rinded and chopped
2 leeks, sliced
4 spring onions, sliced
3 celery sticks, chopped
4 small carrots, sliced
300ml/½ pint/1¼ cups vegetable stock
10ml/2 tsp Dijon mustard
5ml/1 tsp grated lemon rind
45–60ml/3–4 tbsp crème fraîche
salt and black pepper
herby mashed potatoes, to serve

1 Heat the oil in a large flameproof casserole and fry the rabbit pieces until browned all over. Preheat the oven to 190°C/375°F/Gas 5.

2 Add the bacon and vegetables and toss over the heat for 1 minute. Add the stock, mustard, lemon rind and crème fraîche, and seasoning to taste, then bring to the boil.

3 Cover and cook for 35–40 minutes, or until the rabbit is tender (it should take no longer than chicken). Serve with herby mashed potatoes – creamed potatoes well flavoured and coloured with chopped fresh parsley and snipped chives.

ROASTS, PIES & HOT-POTS

Slow-cooked casseroles have a wonderful flavour: try the delicious
Pheasant with Mushrooms, or an easy-to-prepare Turkey
Hot-pot. If you would prefer a roast, make a delicious stuffing for
chicken with celeriac, or prepare it Italian-style with a colourful
tomato coat. Pies are perfect weekend fare, and there are plenty
here to choose from. Try Curried Chicken and Apricot Pie on
your family, or enclose chicken fillets and herby butter in flaky
filo to make delightful individual pastry parcels.

Farmhouse Venison Pie

A simple and satisfying pie – venison in a rich gravy, topped with potato and parsnip mash.

INGREDIENTS

Serves 4

45ml/3 tbsp sunflower oil
1 onion, chopped
1 garlic clove, crushed
3 rashers streaky bacon, rinded and chopped
675g/1½lb minced venison
115g/4oz button mushrooms, chopped
30ml/2 tbsp plain flour
450ml/¾ pint/1⅞ cups beef stock
150ml/¼ pint/⅔ cup ruby port
2 bay leaves
5ml/1 tsp chopped fresh thyme
5ml/1 tsp Dijon mustard
15ml/1 tbsp redcurrant jelly
675g/1½lb potatoes
450g/1lb parsnips
1 egg yolk
50g/2oz/4 tbsp butter
freshly grated nutmeg
45ml/3 tbsp chopped fresh parsley
salt and black pepper

1 Heat the oil in a large frying pan and fry the onion, garlic and bacon for about 5 minutes. Add the venison and mushrooms and cook for a few minutes, stirring, until browned.

2 Stir in the flour and cook for 1–2 minutes, then add the stock, port, herbs, mustard, redcurrant jelly and seasoning. Bring to the boil, cover and simmer for 30–40 minutes, until tender. Spoon into a large pie dish or four individual ovenproof dishes.

3 While the venison and mushroom mixture is cooking, preheat the oven to 200°C/400°F/Gas 6. Cut the potatoes and parsnips into large chunks. Cook in boiling salted water for 20 minutes or until tender. Drain and mash, then beat in the egg yolk, butter, nutmeg, chopped parsley and seasoning.

4 Spread the potato and parsnip mixture over the meat and bake for 30–40 minutes, until piping hot and golden brown. Serve at once.

Chicken and Ham Pie

This domed double-crust pie, filled with a wonderful creamy herb mixture, is ideal for a cold buffet, for picnics or any packed meal.

INGREDIENTS

Serves 8
400g/14oz ready-made shortcrust pastry
800g/1¾lb chicken breast
350g/12oz uncooked gammon
about 60ml/4 tbsp double cream
6 spring onions, finely chopped
15ml/1 tbsp chopped fresh tarragon
10ml/2 tsp chopped fresh thyme
grated rind and juice of ½ large lemon
5ml/1 tsp grated nutmeg
salt and black pepper
beaten egg or milk, to glaze

1 Preheat the oven to 175°C/190°F/ Gas 5. Roll out one-third of the pastry on a floured surface and use it to line a 20cm/8in pie tin 5cm/2in deep. Place on a baking sheet.

2 Mince 115g/4oz of the chicken with the gammon, then mix with the cream, spring onions, herbs, lemon rind, 15ml/1tbsp of the lemon juice and the seasoning to make a soft mixture; add more cream if necessary.

3 Cut the remaining chicken into 1cm/½in pieces and mix with the remaining lemon juice, the nutmeg and seasoning.

4 Make a layer of one-third of the gammon mixture in the pastry base, cover with half the chopped chicken, then add another layer of one-third of the gammon. Add all the remaining chicken followed by the remaining gammon.

5 Dampen the edges of the pastry base. Roll out the remaining pastry to make a lid for the pie.

6 Use the trimmings to make a lattice decoration. Make a small hole in the centre of the pie, brush the top with beaten egg or milk, then bake for about 20 minutes. Reduce the oven temperature to 160°C/325°F/Gas 3 and bake for a further 1–1¼ hours; cover the top with foil if the pastry becomes too brown. Transfer the pie to a wire rack and leave to cool.

Chicken, Leek and Parsley Pie

INGREDIENTS

Serves 4–6

For the pastry
275g/10oz/2½ cups plain flour
pinch of salt
200g/7oz/7/8 cup butter, diced
2 egg yolks

For the filling
3 part-boned chicken breasts
flavouring ingredients (bouquet garni,
    black peppercorns, onion and carrot)
50g/2oz/4 tbsp butter
2 leeks, thinly sliced
50g/2oz Cheddar cheese, grated
25g/1oz Parmesan cheese, finely grated
45ml/3 tbsp chopped fresh parsley
30ml/2 tbsp wholegrain mustard
5ml/1 tsp cornflour
300ml/½ pint/1¼ cups double cream
salt and black pepper
beaten egg, to glaze
mixed green salad, to serve

1 To make the pastry, first sift the flour and salt. Blend together the butter and egg yolks in a food processor until creamy. Add the flour and process until the mixture is just coming together. Add about 15ml/1 tbsp cold water and process for a few seconds more. Turn out on to a lightly floured surface and knead lightly. Wrap in clear film and chill for about 1 hour.

2 Meanwhile, poach the chicken breasts in water to cover, with the flavouring ingredients added, until tender. Leave to cool in the liquid.

3 Preheat the oven to 200°C/400°F/ Gas 6. Divide the pastry into two pieces, one slightly larger than the other. Roll out the larger piece on a lightly floured surface and use to line a 18 x 28cm/7 x 11in baking dish or tin. Prick the base with a fork and bake for 15 minutes. Leave to cool.

4 Lift the cooled chicken from the poaching liquid and discard the skins and bones. Cut the chicken flesh into strips, then set aside.

5 Melt the butter in a frying pan and fry the leeks over a low heat, stirring occasionally, until soft.

6 Stir in the Cheddar, Parmesan and chopped parsley. Spread half the leek mixture over the cooked pastry base, leaving a border all the way round. Cover the leek mixture with the chicken strips, then top with the remaining leek mixture.

7 Mix together the mustard, cornflour and cream in a small bowl. Add seasoning to taste. Pour over the filling.

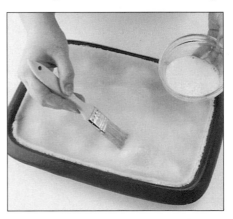

8 Moisten the edges of the cooked pastry base. Roll out the remaining pastry and use to cover the pie. Brush with beaten egg and bake for 30–40 minutes until golden and crisp. Serve hot, cut into square portions, with a mixed green salad.

COOK'S TIP

This pastry is quite fragile and may break; the high fat content, however, means you can patch it together by pressing pieces of pastry trimmings into any cracks.

Chicken Parcels with Herb Butter

INGREDIENTS

Serves 4

4 chicken breast fillets, skinned
150g/5oz/10 tbsp butter, softened
90ml/6 tbsp chopped fresh mixed
    herbs, such as thyme, parsley,
    oregano and rosemary
5ml/1 tsp lemon juice
5 large sheets filo pastry, defrosted
    if frozen
1 egg, beaten
30ml/2 tbsp grated Parmesan cheese
salt and black pepper

1 Season the chicken fillets and fry in 25g/1oz/2 tbsp of the butter to seal and brown lightly. Allow to cool.

2 Preheat the oven to 190°C/375°F/ Gas 5. Put the remaining butter, the herbs, lemon juice and seasoning in a food processor and process until smooth. Melt half the herb butter.

3 Take one sheet of filo pastry and brush with herb butter. Fold the filo pastry sheet in half and brush again with butter. Place a chicken fillet about 2.5cm/1in from the top end.

4 Dot the chicken with a quarter of the remaining herb butter. Fold in the sides of the pastry, then roll up to enclose it completely. Place seam-side down on a lightly greased baking sheet. Repeat with the other chicken fillets.

5 Brush the filo parcels with beaten egg. Cut the last sheet of filo into strips, then scrunch and arrange on top. Brush the parcels once again with the egg glaze, then sprinkle with Parmesan. Bake for about 35–40 minutes, until golden brown. Serve hot.

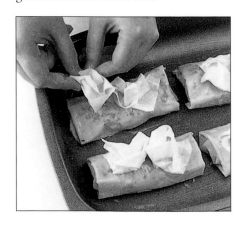

Stoved Chicken

'Stoved' is derived from the French *étouffer* – which means to cook in a covered pot – and originates from the Franco/Scottish 'Alliance' of the seventeenth century.

INGREDIENTS

Serves 4

1kg/2lb potatoes, cut into 5mm/¼in slices
2 large onions, thinly sliced
15ml/1 tbsp chopped fresh thyme
25g/1oz/2 tbsp butter
15ml/1 tbsp oil
2 large slices bacon, chopped
4 large chicken joints, halved
bay leaf
600ml/1 pint/2½ cups chicken stock
salt and black pepper

1 Preheat the oven to 150°C/300°F/ Gas 2. Make a thick layer of half the potato slices in the bottom of a large, heavy casserole, then cover with half the onion. Sprinkle with half the thyme, and seasonings.

COOK'S TIP

Instead of buying large chicken joints and cutting them in half, choose either chicken thighs or chicken drumsticks – or use a mixture of the two.

---

2 Heat the butter and oil in a large frying pan, then brown the bacon and chicken. Using a slotted spoon, transfer the chicken and bacon to the casserole. Reserve the fat in the pan.

3 Sprinkle the remaining thyme and some seasoning over the chicken, then cover with the remaining onion, followed by a neat layer of overlapping potato slices. Sprinkle with seasoning.

4 Pour the stock into the casserole, brush the potatoes with the reserved fat, then cover tightly and cook in the oven for about 2 hours, until the chicken is tender.

5 Preheat the grill. Uncover the casserole and place under the grill and cook until the slices of potato are beginning to brown and crisp. Serve hot.

Pot-roast of Venison

INGREDIENTS

Serves 4–5

1.75kg/4– 4½lb boned joint of
  venison
75ml/5 tbsp oil
4 cloves
8 black peppercorns, lightly crushed
12 juniper berries, lightly crushed
250ml/8fl oz/1 cup full-bodied red
  wine
115g/4oz lightly smoked streaky
  bacon, chopped
2 onions, finely chopped
2 carrots, chopped
150g/5oz large mushrooms, sliced
15ml/1 tbsp plain flour
250ml/8fl oz/1 cup veal stock
30ml/2 tbsp redcurrant jelly
salt and black pepper

1 Put the venison in a bowl, add half
the oil, the spices and wine, cover
and leave in a cool place for 24 hours,
turning the meat occasionally.

2 Preheat the oven to 160°C/325°F/
Gas 3. Remove the venison from
the bowl and pat dry. Reserve the
marinade. Heat the remaining oil in a
shallow pan, then brown the venison
evenly. Transfer to a plate.

3 Stir the bacon, onions, carrots and
mushrooms into the pan and cook
for about 5 minutes. Stir in the flour
and cook for 2 minutes, then remove
from the heat and stir in the marinade,
stock, redcurrant jelly and seasoning.
Return to the heat, bring to the boil,
stirring, then simmer for 2–3 minutes.

4 Transfer the venison and sauce to
a casserole, cover and cook in the
oven, turning the joint occasionally,
for about 3 hours, until tender.

Pheasant with Mushrooms

INGREDIENTS

Serves 4

1 pheasant, jointed
250ml/8fl oz/1 cup red wine
45ml/3 tbsp oil
60ml/4 tbsp Spanish sherry vinegar
1 large onion, chopped
2 slices smoked bacon, cut into strips
350g/12oz chestnut mushrooms,
  sliced
3 anchovy fillets, soaked for 10
  minutes and drained
350ml/12fl oz/1½ cups game, veal or
  chicken stock
bouquet garni
salt and black pepper

1 Place the pheasant in a dish, add
the wine, half the oil and half the
vinegar, and scatter over half the
onion. Season, then cover and leave in
a cool place for 8–12 hours, turning
the pheasant occasionally.

2 Preheat the oven to 160°C/325°F/
Gas 3. Lift the pheasant from the
dish, pat dry. Reserve the marinade.

3 Heat the remaining oil in a flameproof casserole, then brown the
pheasant joints. Transfer to a plate.

4 Add the bacon and remaining
onion to the casserole and cook
until the onion is soft. Stir in the mushrooms and cook for about 3 minutes.

5 Stir in the anchovies and remain-
ing vinegar, boil until reduced.
Add the marinade, cook for 2 minutes,
then add the stock and bouquet garni.
Return the pheasant to the casserole,
cover and bake for about 1½ hours.
Transfer the pheasant to a serving dish.
Boil the cooking juices to reduce.
Discard the bouquet garni. Pour over
the pheasant and serve at once.

Cornish Chicken Pie

Since this dish comes from Cornwall, typically cream is used in the filling.

INGREDIENTS

Serves 4

50g/2oz/4 tbsp butter
4 chicken legs
1 onion, finely chopped
150ml/¼ pint/⅔ cup milk
150ml/¼ pint/⅔ cup soured cream
4 spring onions, quartered
20g/¾oz fresh parsley leaves, finely chopped
225g/8oz ready-made puff pastry
120ml/4fl oz/½ cup double cream
2 eggs, beaten, plus extra for glazing
salt and black pepper

1 Melt the butter in a heavy-based, shallow pan, then brown the chicken legs. Transfer to a plate.

2 Add the chopped onion to the pan and cook until softened but not browned. Stir the milk, soured cream, spring onions, parsley and seasoning into the pan, bring to the boil, then simmer for a couple of minutes, stirrring occasionally.

3 Return the chicken to the pan with any juices, then cover tightly and cook very gently for about 30 minutes. Transfer the chicken and sauce mixture to a 1.2 litre/2 pint/5 cup pie dish and leave to cool.

4 Meanwhile, roll out the pastry until about 2cm/¾in larger all round than the top of the pie dish. Leave the pastry to relax while the chicken is cooling.

5 Preheat the oven to 220°C/425°F/Gas 7. Cut off a narrow strip around the edge of the pastry, then place the strip on the edge of the pie dish. Moisten the strip, then cover the dish with the pastry. Press the edges together.

6 Make a hole in the centre of the pastry and insert a small funnel of foil. Brush the pastry with beaten egg, then bake for 15–20 minutes.

7 Reduce the oven temperature to 180°C/350°F/Gas 4. Mix the cream and eggs, then pour into the pie through the funnel. Shake the pie to distribute the cream, then return to the oven for 5–10 minutes. Remove the pie from the oven and leave in a warm place for 5–10 minutes before serving, or cool completely if serving cold.

Normandy Pheasant

Cider, apples and cream make this a rich and flavoursome dish.

INGREDIENTS

Serves 4

2 oven-ready pheasants
15ml/1 tbsp olive oil
25g/1oz/2 tbsp butter
60ml/4 tbsp Calvados
450ml/¾ pint/1⅞ cups dry cider
bouquet garni
3 Cox's Pippins apples, peeled, cored
  and thickly sliced
150ml/¼ pint/⅔ cup double cream
salt and black pepper
thyme sprigs, to garnish

1 Preheat the oven to 160°C/325°F/ Gas 3. Joint both pheasants into four pieces using a large sharp knife. Discard the backbones and knuckles.

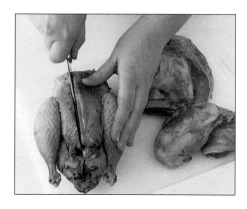

2 Heat the oil and butter in a large flameproof casserole. Working in two batches, add the pheasant pieces to the casserole and brown them over a high heat. Return all the pheasant pieces to the casserole.

3 Standing well back, pour over the Calvados and set it alight. When the flames have subsided, pour in the cider, then add the bouquet garni and seasoning and bring to the boil. Cover and cook for 30 minutes.

4 Tuck the apple slices around the pheasant. Cover and cook for 5–10 minutes, or until the pheasant is tender. Transfer the pheasant and apple to a warmed serving plate. Keep warm.

5 Remove the bouquet garni, then reduce the sauce by half to a syrupy consistency. Stir in the cream and simmer for a further 2–3 minutes until thickened. Taste the sauce and adjust the seasoning. Spoon the sauce over the pheasant and serve hot, garnished with thyme sprigs.

Chicken and Mushroom Pie

INGREDIENTS

Serves 6

15g/½oz dried porcini mushrooms
50g/2oz/4 tbsp butter
15g/½oz/2 tbsp plain flour
250ml/8fl oz/1 cup hot chicken stock
50ml/2fl oz/¼ cup single cream or
  milk
1 onion, coarsely chopped
2 carrots, sliced
2 celery sticks, coarsely chopped
50g/2oz fresh mushrooms, quartered
450g/1lb cooked chicken meat,
  cubed
50g/2oz fresh or frozen peas
salt and black pepper
beaten egg, to glaze

For the pastry

225g/8oz/2 cups plain flour
1.25ml/¼ tsp salt
115g/4oz/½ cup cold butter,
  diced
65g/2½oz/⅓ cup white cooking fat,
  diced
60–120ml/4–8 tbsp iced water

1 To make the pastry, sift the flour and salt into a bowl. With a pastry blender or two knives, cut in the butter and cooking fat until the mixture resembles breadcrumbs. Sprinkle with 90ml/6 tbsp iced water and mix until the dough holds together. If the dough is too crumbly, add a little more water, 15ml/1 tbsp at a time. Gather the dough into a ball and flatten into a round. Place in a sealed polythene bag and chill for at least 30 minutes.

2 Place the porcini mushrooms in a small bowl. Add hot water to cover and leave to soak for about 30 minutes, until soft. Lift out of the water with a slotted spoon to leave any grit behind and drain on kitchen paper. Discard the soaking water. Preheat the oven to 190°C/375°F/Gas 5.

3 Melt half of the butter in a heavy-based saucepan. Whisk in the flour and cook until bubbling, whisking constantly. Add the warm stock and cook over a medium heat, whisking, until the mixture boils. Cook for 2–3 minutes more, then whisk in the cream or milk. Season with salt and pepper and set aside.

4 Heat the remaining butter in a large non-stick frying pan until sizzling. Add the onion and carrots and cook for about 5 minutes, until softened. Add the celery and fresh mushrooms and cook for a further 5 minutes. Stir in the cooked chicken, peas and drained porcini mushrooms.

5 Add the chicken mixture to the cream sauce and stir to mix. Taste for seasoning. Turn into a 2.5 litre/ 4 pint rectangular baking dish.

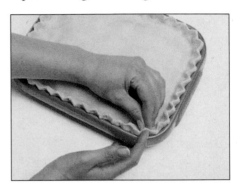

6 Roll out the dough to about a 3mm/⅛in thickness. Cut out a rectangle about 2.5cm/1in larger all around than the dish. Lay the rectangle of dough over the filling. Make a decorative edge by pushing the index finger of one hand between the thumb and index finger of the other.

7 Cut several slits in the pastry to allow steam to escape then brush the pastry with the beaten egg.

8 Press together the pastry trimmings and roll out again. Cut into thin strips and lay them over the pastry lid. Glaze again. If liked, roll small balls of dough and arrange them in the "windows" in the lattice.

9 Bake for about 30 minutes, until the pastry is browned. Serve the pie hot from the dish.

Mixed Game Pie

INGREDIENTS

Serves 4

450g/1lb game meat, off the bone
    (plus the carcasses and bones)
1 small onion, halved
2 bay leaves
2 carrots, halved
few black peppercorns
15ml/1 tbsp oil
75g/3oz streaky bacon pieces, rinded
    and chopped
15ml/1 tbsp plain flour
45ml/3 tbsp sweet sherry or Madeira
10ml/2 tsp ground ginger
grated rind and juice of ½ orange
350g/12oz ready-made puff pastry
egg or milk, to glaze
salt and black pepper

1 Place the carcasses and bones in a pan, with any giblets and half the onion, the bay leaves, carrots and black peppercorns. Cover with water and bring to the boil. Simmer until reduced to about 300ml/½ pint/1¼ cups, then strain the stock, ready to use.

2 Cut the game meat into even size pieces. Fry the remaining onion, chopped, in the oil until softened. Then add the bacon and meat and fry quickly to seal. Sprinkle on the flour and stir until beginning to brown. Gradually add the stock, stirring as it thickens, then add the sherry or Madeira, ginger, orange rind and juice, and seasoning. Simmer for 20 minutes.

3 Transfer to a 900ml/1½ pint/3¾ cup pie dish and allow to cool slightly. Put a pie funnel in the centre of the filling to help hold up the pastry.

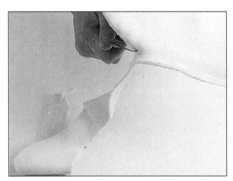

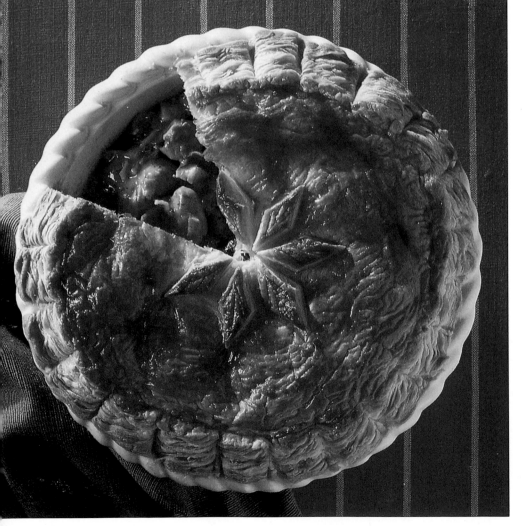

4 Preheat the oven to 220°C/425°F/ Gas 7. Roll out the pastry to 2.5cm/ 1in larger than the dish. Cut off a 1cm/½in strip all round. Damp the rim of the dish and press on the strip of pastry. Damp again and then lift the pastry carefully over the pie, sealing the edges well at the rim. Trim off the excess pastry, use to decorate the top, then brush the pie with egg or milk.

5 Bake for 15 minutes, then reduce the heat to 190°C/375°F/Gas 5, for a further 25–30 minutes. Serve with redcurrant, or sage and apple, jelly.

Roast Chicken with Celeriac

INGREDIENTS

Serves 4

1.6kg/3½lb chicken
15g/½oz/1 tbsp butter

For the stuffing

450g/1lb celeriac, chopped
25g/1oz/2 tbsp butter
3 slices bacon, chopped
1 onion, finely chopped
leaves from 1 thyme sprig, chopped
leaves from 1 small tarragon sprig,
   chopped
30ml/2 tbsp chopped fresh parsley
75g/3oz/1½ cups fresh brown
   breadcrumbs
dash of Worcestershire sauce
1 egg
salt and black pepper

1 To make the stuffing, cook the celeriac in boiling water until tender. Drain well and chop finely.

2 Heat the butter in a saucepan, then gently cook the bacon and onion until the onion is soft. Stir the celeriac and herb leaves into the pan and cook, stirring occasionally, for 2–3 minutes. Meanwhile, preheat the oven to 200°C/400°F/Gas 6.

> **COOK'S TIP**
>
> Roll any excess stuffing into small balls and bake in a buttered ovenproof dish with the chicken for 20–30 minutes until golden brown.

3 Remove the pan from the heat and stir in the fresh breadcrumbs, Worcestershire sauce, seasoning and sufficient egg to bind. Use to stuff the neck end of the chicken. Season the bird's skin, then rub with the butter.

4 Roast the chicken, basting occasionally with the juices, for 1¼–1½ hours, until the juices run clear when the thickest part of the leg is pierced.

5 Turn off the oven, prop the door open slightly and allow the chicken to rest for 10 minutes before carving.

Chicken, Carrot and Leek Parcels

These intriguing parcels may sound a bit fiddly for everyday, but they take very little time and you can freeze them – ready to cook gently from frozen.

INGREDIENTS

Serves 4

4 chicken fillets or boneless breast
  portions
2 small leeks, sliced
2 carrots, grated
4 stoned black olives, chopped
1 garlic clove, crushed
15–30ml/1–2 tbsp olive oil
8 anchovy fillets
salt and black pepper
black olives and herb sprigs, to garnish

1 Preheat the oven to 200°C/400°F/ Gas 6. Season the chicken well.

2 Divide the leeks equally among four sheets of greased greaseproof paper, about 23cm/9in square. Place a piece of chicken on top of each.

3 Mix the carrots, olives, garlic and oil together. Season lightly and place on top of the chicken portions. Top each with two of the anchovy fillets, then carefully wrap up each parcel, making sure the paper folds are underneath and the carrot mixture on top.

4 Bake for 20 minutes and serve hot, in the paper, garnished with black olives and herb sprigs.

Chicken in a Tomato Coat

INGREDIENTS

Serves 4–6

1.5–1.75kg/3½–4lb free-range chicken
1 small onion
knob of butter
75ml/5 tbsp ready-made tomato sauce
30ml/2 tbsp chopped, mixed fresh
  herbs, such as parsley, tarragon, sage,
  basil and marjoram, or 10ml/2 tsp
  dried
small glass of dry white wine
2–3 small tomatoes, sliced
olive oil
little cornflour (optional)
salt and black pepper

1 Preheat the oven to 190°C/375°F/ Gas 5. Wash and wipe dry the chicken and place in a roasting tin. Place the onion, a knob of butter and some seasoning inside the chicken.

2 Spread most of the tomato sauce over the chicken and sprinkle with half the herbs and some seasoning. Pour the wine into the roasting tin.

3 Cover with foil, then roast for 1½ hours, basting occasionally. Remove the foil, spread with the remaining sauce and the sliced tomatoes and drizzle with oil. Continue cooking for a further 20–30 minutes, or until the chicken is cooked through.

4 Sprinkle the remaining herbs over the chicken, then carve into portions. Thicken the sauce with a little cornflour if you wish. Serve hot.

Rabbit with Mustard

INGREDIENTS

Serves 4

15ml/1 tbsp plain flour
15ml/1 tbsp English mustard powder
4 large rabbit joints
25g/1oz/2 tbsp butter
30ml/2 tbsp oil
1 onion, finely chopped
150ml/¼ pint/⅔ cup beer
300ml/½ pint/1¼ cups chicken or veal
　stock
15ml/1 tbsp tarragon vinegar
30ml/2 tbsp dark brown sugar
10–15ml/2–3 tsp prepared English
　mustard
salt and black pepper

To finish

50g/2oz/4 tbsp butter
30ml/2 tbsp oil
50g/2 oz/1 cup fresh breadcrumbs
15ml/1 tbsp snipped fresh chives
15ml/1 tbsp chopped fresh tarragon

1 Preheat the oven to 160°C/325°F/
Gas 3. Mix the flour and mustard
powder together, then put on a plate.

2 Dip the rabbit joints in the flour
mixture, reserve excess flour. Heat
the butter and oil in a heavy flameproof casserole, then brown the rabbit.
Transfer to a plate. Stir in the onion
and cook until soft.

3 Stir in any reserved flour mixture
and cook for 1 minute, then stir in
the beer, stock and vinegar. Bring to
the boil and add the sugar and pepper.
Simmer for 2 minutes.

4 Return the rabbit and any juices
that have collected on the plate, to
the casserole, cover tightly and cook in
the oven for 1 hour.

5 Stir the prepared mustard and salt
to taste into the casserole, cover
again and cook over a low heat for a
further 15 minutes.

6 To finish, heat together the butter
and oil in a frying pan and fry the
breadcrumbs, stirring frequently, until
golden, then stir in the herbs. Transfer
the rabbit to a warmed serving dish,
sprinkle over the breadcrumb mixture
and serve hot.

Turkey Hot-pot

INGREDIENTS

Serves 4

115g/4oz dried kidney beans, soaked
　overnight and drained
40g/1½oz/3 tbsp butter
2 herby pork sausages
450g/1lb turkey casserole meat
3 leeks, sliced
2 carrots, finely chopped
4 tomatoes, chopped
10–15ml/2–3 tsp tomato purée
bouquet garni
400ml/14fl oz/1⅔ cups chicken
　stock
salt and black pepper

1 Cook the beans in boiling water
for 40 minutes, then drain well.

2 Meanwhile, heat the butter in a
flameproof casserole, then cook
the sausages until browned and the fat
runs. Drain on kitchen paper, stir the
turkey into the casserole and cook
until lightly browned all over, then
transfer to a bowl using a slotted
spoon. Stir the leeks and carrot into
the casserole and brown lightly.

3 Add the tomatoes and tomato
purée and simmer gently for
about 5 minutes.

4 Chop the sausages and return to
the casserole with the beans,
turkey, bouquet garni, stock and seasoning. Cover and cook gently for
about 1¼ hours, until the beans are
tender and there is very little liquid.

Curried Chicken and Apricot Pie

This pie is unusually sweet-sour and very moreish. Use boneless turkey instead of chicken if you wish, or even some leftovers from a roast turkey – the dark, moist leg meat is best.

INGREDIENTS

Serves 6

30ml/2 tbsp sunflower oil
1 large onion, chopped
450g/1lb boneless chicken, roughly chopped
15ml/1 tbsp curry paste or powder
30ml/2 tbsp apricot or peach chutney
115g/4oz/⅔ cup ready-to-eat dried apricots, halved
115g/4oz cooked carrots, sliced
5ml/1 tsp mixed dried herbs
60ml/4 tbsp crème fraîche
350g/12oz ready-made shortcrust pastry
little egg or milk, to glaze
salt and black pepper

1 Heat the oil in a large pan and fry the onion and chicken until just colouring. Add the curry paste or powder and fry for 2 minutes more.

2 Add the chutney, apricots, carrots, herbs and crème fraîche to the pan with seasoning. Mix well and then transfer to a deep 900ml–1.2 litre/1½–2 pint/4–5 cup ovenproof pie dish.

3 Roll out the pastry to 2.5cm/1in wider than the pie dish. Cut a strip of pastry from the edge. Damp the rim of the dish, press on the strip, then brush these strips with water and place the sheet of pastry on top, press to seal.

4 Preheat the oven to 190°C/375°F/ Gas 5. Trim off any excess pastry and use to make an attractive pattern on the top if you wish. Brush all over with beaten egg or milk and bake for 40 minutes, until crisp and golden.

Moroccan Spiced Roast Poussin

INGREDIENTS 🍎

Serves 4

75g/3oz/1½ cups cooked long grain rice
1 small onion, chopped finely
finely grated rind and juice of 1 lemon
30ml/2 tbsp chopped mint
45ml/3 tbsp chopped dried apricots
30ml/2 tbsp natural yogurt
10ml/2 tsp ground turmeric
10ml/2 tsp ground cumin
2 x 450g/1lb poussin
salt and black pepper
lemon slices and mint sprigs, to garnish

1 Preheat the oven to 200°C/400°F/ Gas 6. Mix together the rice, onion, lemon rind, mint, and apricots. Stir in half each of the lemon juice, yogurt, turmeric, cumin, and salt and pepper.

2 Stuff the poussin with the rice mix- ture at the neck end only. Any spare stuffing can be served separately. Place the birds on a rack in a roasting pan.

3 Mix together the remaining lemon juice, yogurt, turmeric, and cumin, then brush this over the poussin. Cover loosely with foil and roast in the oven for 30 minutes.

4 Remove the foil and roast the poussin for a further 15 minutes, or until golden brown and the juices run clear, not pink, when pierced.

5 Cut the poussin in half with a sharp knife or poultry shears, and serve with the reserved rice. Garnish with lemon slices and fresh mint.

> — COOK'S TIP —
>
> If you aren't using leftover rice, but cook- ing it especially for this recipe, make sure the rice has cooled completely before adding to the other stuffing ingredients.

Sticky Ginger Chicken

INGREDIENTS 🍎

Serves 4

30ml/2 tbsp lemon juice
30ml/2 tbsp brown sugar
5ml/1 tsp grated fresh ginger root
10ml/2 tsp soy sauce
8 chicken drumsticks, skinned
black pepper

> — VARIATION —
>
> They are not as low in fat, but skinless duck breasts would be equally good in this recipe. Cook them until they are still very slightly pink in the centre.

1 Mix together the lemon juice, sugar, ginger, soy sauce, and pepper.

2 With a sharp knife, slash the chicken drumsticks about three times through the thickest part, then toss the chicken in the glaze.

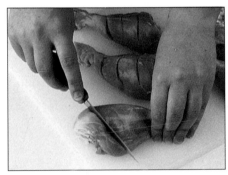

3 Cook the chicken on a grill, or barbecue, turning occasionally and brushing with the glaze, until the chicken is golden and the juices run clear, not pink, when pierced. Serve on a bed of lettuce, with crusty bread.

Poussin with Raisin Stuffing

INGREDIENTS

Serves 4

250ml/8fl oz/1 cup port
115g/4oz/²⁄₃ cup raisins
15ml/1 tbsp walnut oil
75g/3oz mushrooms, finely chopped
1 large celery stick, finely chopped
1 small onion, chopped
50g/2oz/1 cup fresh white
   breadcrumbs
50g/2oz/½ cup chopped walnuts
15ml/1 tbsp each chopped fresh basil
   and parsley
2.5ml/½ tsp dried thyme
75g/3oz/6 tbsp butter, melted
4 poussin
salt and black pepper
salad and cherry tomatoes, to serve

1 Preheat the oven to 180°C/350°F/
Gas 4. Place the port and raisins in
a bowl and soak for about 20 minutes.

2 Meanwhile, heat the oil in a frying
pan. Add the mushrooms, celery,
onion and 1.25ml/¼ tsp salt and cook
over a low heat for 8–10 minutes, until
softened. Leave to cool slightly.

3 Drain the raisins, reserving the
port. Combine the raisins,
breadcrumbs, walnuts, basil, parsley
and thyme in a large bowl. Stir in the
mushroom and onion mixture and
50g/2oz/4 tbsp of the butter. Add salt
and pepper to taste.

4 Fill the cavity of each poussin with
the stuffing mixture. Do not pack
down. Tie the legs together, looping the
tail with string to enclose the stuffing.

5 Brush each the poussin with the
remaining butter and place in a
baking dish just large enough to hold
the birds comfortably. Pour over the
reserved port.

6 Roast for about 1 hour, basting
occasionally. To test whether they
are cooked, pierce the thigh with a
skewer: the juices should run clear.
Serve accompanied by salad and cherry
tomatoes, with the cooking juices
poured over each bird.

French-style Pot-roast Poussin

INGREDIENTS

Serves 4

15ml/1 tbsp olive oil
1 onion, sliced
1 large garlic clove, sliced
50g/2oz/½ cup diced lightly smoked
  bacon
2 fresh poussin (just under 450g/1lb
  each)
30ml/2 tbsp melted butter
2 baby celery hearts, each cut into 4
8 baby carrots
2 small courgettes, cut into chunks
8 small new potatoes
600ml/1 pint/2½ cups chicken stock
150ml/¼ pint/⅔ cup dry white wine
1 bay leaf
2 fresh thyme sprigs
2 fresh rosemary sprigs
15ml/1 tbsp butter, softened
15ml/1 tbsp plain flour
salt and black pepper
fresh herbs, to garnish

1 Preheat the oven to 190°C/375°F/
Gas 5. Heat the olive oil in a large
flameproof casserole and add the onion,
garlic and bacon. Sauté for 5–6 minutes, until the onions have softened.

2 Brush the poussin with a little of
the melted butter and season well.
Lay on top of the onion mixture and
arrange the prepared vegetables around
them. Pour the chicken stock and wine
around the birds and add the herbs.

3 Cover, bake for 20 minutes, then
remove the lid and brush the birds
with the remaining butter. Bake for a
further 25–30 minutes until golden.

4 Transfer the poussin to a warmed
serving platter and cut each in half
with poultry shears or scissors. Remove
the vegetables with a draining spoon
and arrange them round the birds.
Cover with foil and keep warm.

5 Discard the herbs from the pan
juices. In a bowl mix together the
butter and flour to form a paste. Bring
the liquid in the pan to the boil and
then whisk in teaspoonfuls of the paste
until thickened. Season the sauce and
serve with the poussin and vegetables,
garnished with fresh herbs.

Coq au Vin

INGREDIENTS

Serves 4

45ml/3 tbsp plain flour
1.5kg/3lb chicken, cut into 8 joints
15ml/1 tbsp olive oil
50g/2oz/4 tbsp butter
20 baby onions
75g/3oz piece streaky bacon without rind, diced
about 20 button mushrooms
30ml/2 tbsp brandy
75cl bottle red Burgundy wine
bouquet garni
3 garlic cloves
5ml/1 tsp soft light brown sugar
15ml/1 tbsp butter, softened
15ml/1 tbsp plain flour
salt and black pepper
15ml/1 tbsp chopped fresh parsley and croûtons, to garnish

1 Place the flour and seasoning in a large plastic bag and shake each chicken joint in it until lightly coated. Heat the oil and butter in a large flameproof casserole. Add the onions and bacon and sauté for 3–4 minutes, until the onions have browned lightly. Add the mushrooms and fry for 2 minutes. Remove with a slotted spoon into a bowl and reserve.

2 Add the chicken pieces to the hot oil and cook until browned on all sides, about 5–6 minutes. Pour in the brandy and (standing well back from the pan) carefully light it with a match, then shake the pan gently until the flames subside. Pour on the wine, add the bouquet garni, garlic, sugar and seasoning.

3 Bring to the boil, cover and simmer for 1 hour, stirring occasionally. Return the reserved onions, bacon and mushrooms to the casserole, cover and cook for a further 30 minutes.

4 Lift out the chicken, vegetables and bacon with a draining spoon and arrange on a warmed dish.

5 Remove the bouquet garni and boil the liquid rapidly for 2 minutes to reduce slightly. Cream the butter and flour together and whisk in teaspoonfuls of the mixture until the liquid has thickened slightly. Pour this sauce over the chicken and serve garnished with parsley and croûtons.

INDEX

Apples: guinea fowl with cider and apples, 63
Normandy pheasant, 81
pheasant with apples, 54
Apricots: curried chicken and apricot pie, 92
Moroccan spiced roast poussin, 90
Avocado: lemon chicken with guacamole sauce, 52

Bacon: chicken, bacon and corn kebabs, 16
chicken with herbs and lentils, 19
coq au vin, 95
stoved chicken, 77
Blackberries: duck breasts with blackberries, 68
Broad beans: chicken, pepper and bean stew, 60

Cabbage: chicken with red cabbage, 38
Cajun chicken Jambalaya, 15
Cajun-spiced chicken, 51
Cannellini beans: Tuscan chicken, 67
Caribbean chicken kebabs, 31
Carrots: chicken, carrot and leek parcels, 86
Cashew nuts: Chinese chicken with cashew nuts, 40
Casseroles and stews: chicken, pepper and bean stew, 60
coq au vin, 95
country cider hot-pot, 58
pheasant with mushrooms, 78
spring rabbit casserole, 68
turkey hot-pot, 88
Celeriac: roast chicken with celeriac, 85
Cheese: Hampshire farmhouse flan, 42
turkey with yellow pepper sauce, 57
Chicken: Cajun chicken Jambalaya, 15
Cajun-spiced chicken, 51
Caribbean chicken kebabs, 31
chicken and ham pie, 73
chicken and mushroom pie, 82
chicken, bacon and corn kebabs, 16
chicken biryani, 43
chicken, carrot and leek parcels, 86
chicken in a tomato coat, 86
chicken in creamy orange sauce, 37
chicken in green sauce, 66
chicken, leek and parsley pie, 74
chicken parcels with herb butter, 76
chicken, pepper and bean stew, 60
chicken with herbs and lentils, 19
chicken with honey and grapefruit, 28
chicken with lemon and herbs, 38
chicken with red cabbage, 38
chicken with white wine and olives, 32
chilli-chicken couscous, 20
Chinese chicken with cashew nuts, 40
Chinese-style chicken salad, 22
coq au vin, 95
Cornish chicken pie, 80
coronation chicken, 64
crispy chicken with garlicky rice, 28
curried chicken and apricot pie, 92
Hampshire farmhouse flan, 42

honey and orange glazed chicken, 24
Italian chicken, 24
lemon chicken with guacamole sauce, 52
minted yogurt chicken, 34
oat-coated chicken with sage, 56
oven-fried chicken, 36
roast chicken with celeriac, 85
sticky ginger chicken, 90
stoved chicken, 77
Tandoori chicken kebabs, 40
Thai chicken and vegetable stir-fry, 26
Tuscan chicken, 67
Chilli: chicken biryani, 43
chilli-chicken couscous, 20
Chinese chicken with cashew nuts, 40
Chinese-style chicken salad, 22
Cider: cider-baked rabbit, 54
country cider hot-pot, 58
guinea fowl with cider and apples, 63
Normandy pheasant, 81
Coq au vin, 95
Cornish chicken pie, 80
Coronation chicken, 64
Country cider hot-pot, 58
Couscous: chilli-chicken couscous, 20
Cranberries: venison with cranberry sauce, 48
Crispy chicken with garlicky rice, 28
Crumbed turkey steaks, 58
Curry: coronation chicken, 64
curried chicken and apricot pie, 92

Duck: duck breasts with blackberries, 68
duck breasts with orange sauce, 46
duck with Cumberland sauce, 64
mandarin sesame duck, 34

Farmhouse venison pie, 72
French-style pot-roast poussin, 94

Game: mixed game pie, 84
Garlic: crispy chicken with garlicky rice, 28
Ginger: sticky ginger chicken, 90
Grapefruit: chicken with honey and grapefruit, 28
Grapes: poussin with grapes in vermouth, 62
Guinea fowl with cider and apples, 63

Ham: Cajun chicken Jambalaya, 15
chicken and ham pie, 73
Hampshire farmhouse flan, 42
Herbs: chicken in a tomato coat, 86
chicken parcels with herb butter, 76
chicken with herbs and lentils, 19
chicken with lemon and herbs, 38
oven-fried chicken, 36
Honey: chicken with honey and grapefruit, 28
honey and orange glazed chicken, 24

Italian chicken, 24

Kebabs: Caribbean chicken kebabs, 31

chicken, bacon and corn kebabs, 16
Tandoori chicken kebabs, 40
Kidney beans: turkey and bean bake, 20
turkey hot-pot, 88

Leeks: chicken, carrot and leek parcels, 86
chicken, leek and parsley pie, 74
Lemon: chicken with lemon and herbs, 38
lemon chicken with guacamole sauce, 52
Lentils: chicken with herbs and lentils, 19

Mandarin sesame duck, 34
Mange-tout: stir-fried turkey with mange-tout, 23
Mangoes: Caribbean chicken kebabs, 31
Meat loaf, turkey, 32
Minted yogurt chicken, 34
Mixed game pie, 84
Moroccan spiced roast poussin, 90
Mushrooms: chicken and mushroom pie, 82
pheasant with mushrooms, 78
Mustard: rabbit with mustard, 88

Normandy pheasant, 81
Normandy roast chicken, 46

Oat-coated chicken with sage, 56
Olives: chicken with white wine and olives, 32
Oranges: chicken in creamy orange sauce, 37
duck breasts with orange sauce, 46
duck with Cumberland sauce, 64
honey and orange glazed chicken, 24
mandarin sesame duck, 34
Oven-fried chicken, 36

Parsley: chicken, leek and parsley pie, 74
Normandy roast chicken, 46
rabbit with parsley sauce, 50
Parsnips: farmhouse venison pie, 72
Pasta: Italian chicken, 24
pasta with turkey and tomatoes, 27
turkey pastitsio, 18
turkey spirals, 30
Peppers: chicken, pepper and bean stew, 60
turkey with yellow pepper sauce, 57
Tuscan chicken, 67
Pheasant: Normandy pheasant, 81
pheasant with apples, 54
pheasant with mushrooms, 78
Pies: chicken and ham pie, 73
chicken and mushroom pie, 82
chicken, leek and parsley pie, 74
Cornish chicken pie, 80
curried chicken and apricot pie, 92
farmhouse venison pie, 72
mixed game pie, 84
Pot-roast: French-style pot-roast poussin, 94
pot-roast of venison, 78
Potatoes: farmhouse venison pie, 72

stoved chicken, 77
Poussins: French-style pot-roast poussin, 94
Moroccan spiced roast poussin, 90
poussin with grapes in vermouth, 62
poussin with raisin stuffing, 93
spatchcocked devilled poussin, 14

Rabbit: cider-baked rabbit, 54
country cider hot-pot, 58
rabbit with mustard, 88
rabbit with parsley sauce, 50
spring rabbit casserole, 68
Raisins: poussin with raisin stuffing, 93
Rice: chicken biryani, 43
crispy chicken with garlicky rice, 28
Moroccan spiced roast poussin, 90
Roast chicken with celeriac, 85

Sage: oat-coated chicken with sage, 56
Sausages: Cajun chicken Jambalaya, 15
turkey hot-pot, 88
Sesame seeds: mandarin sesame duck, 34
Soured cream: Cornish chicken pie, 80
lemon chicken with guacamole sauce, 52
turkey sticks with soured cream dip, 16
Spatchcocked devilled poussin, 14
Spring rabbit casserole, 68
Stir-fry: stir-fried turkey with mange-tout, 23
Thai chicken and vegetable stir-fry, 26
Stoved chicken, 77
Sweetcorn: chicken, bacon and corn kebabs, 16
chicken, pepper and bean stew, 60

Tandoori chicken kebabs, 40
Thai chicken and vegetable stir-fry, 26
Tomatoes: chicken in a tomato coat, 86
pasta with turkey and tomatoes, 27
Turkey: crumbed turkey steaks, 58
pasta with turkey and tomatoes, 27
stir-fried turkey with mange-tout, 23
turkey and bean bake, 20
turkey hot-pot, 88
turkey meat loaf, 32
turkey pastitsio, 18
turkey spirals, 30
turkey sticks with soured cream dip, 16
turkey with yellow pepper sauce, 57
Tuscan chicken, 67

Vegetables: Thai chicken and vegetable stir-fry, 26
Venison: farmhouse venison pie, 72
pot-roast of venison, 78
venison with cranberry sauce, 48

Watercress: chicken in green sauce, 66
Hampshire farmhouse flan, 42
Wine: chicken with white wine and olives, 32
coq au vin, 95
poussin with grapes in vermouth, 62

Yogurt: minted yogurt chicken, 34